DECADES

Roxy Music
in the 1970s

Dave Thompson

sonicbondpublishing.com

Sonicbond Publishing Limited
www.sonicbondpublishing.co.uk
Email: info@sonicbondpublishing.co.uk

First Published in the United Kingdom 2022
First Published in the United States 2022

British Library Cataloguing in Publication Data:
A Catalogue record for this book is available from the British Library

ISBN 978-1-78952-180-1

Typeset in ITC Garamond & ITC Avant Garde
Printed and bound in England

Graphic design and typesetting: Full Moon Media

DECADES

Roxy Music
in the 1970s

Dave Thompson

sonicbondpublishing.com

Acknowledgements

Thanks, as always, to Amy Hanson, for patiently sitting through more demonstrations of the 'Sombre Reptiles' dance than anybody has a need to; to Jo-Ann Greene, for advice and suggestions that I may or may not have acted upon; to Jon Mills, Pat Prince, Billy James, Todd Nakamine, Bill Rieflin, and to Stephen at Sonicbond books for giving this the go-ahead.

For the interviews, conversation and correspondence that built up over the years to give this book so much of its flavour, much gratitude to Phil Manzanera, Andy Mackay, Bill McCormick, Sal Maida, Gavin Bryars, Nico, Philip Rambow, Davy O'List, Steve Severin, Kevin Godley, Chris Spedding, John Wetton, Jim McCarty, Chris Charlesworth, Greg Shaw, Ian MacDonald and John Foxx.

Elements of many of these have appeared in past books of mine, most notably *Growing Up With John's Children* (self-published, 1982), *Sparks – #1 Songs In Heaven* (Cherry Red, 2009), *Children of the Revolution: The Glam Rock Story* (Cherry Red, 2010), *June 1st 1974: Kevin Ayers, John Cale, Nico, Eno, Mike Oldfield and Robert Wyatt: The Greatest Supergroup of the Seventies* (Createspace, 2013), and *The Avant-Garde Woodstock – the International Carnival of Experimental Sound, 1972* (Lulu, 2017). At last, they have found the home they always yearned for. An appreciative nod to the army of journalists who documented Roxy's career through the 1970s, and whose writings are acknowledged throughout the text.

Finally, to George and Trevor, for not walking across the keyboard as I wrote, and Oliver, who has taken to doing the complete opposite; snails and fishies; the gremlins that live in the heat pump; Karen and Todd; Jen W; Kate Poole, and to all the old friends who lived some – if not most – of these pages with me.

Author's note

Interviews quoted in the text are from my own conversations with musicians and associates unless otherwise noted.

DECADES | Roxy Music in the 1970s

Contents

Introduction

The story of Roxy Music spans the 1970s like no other. The first commercially-available recording by any future member of the band – a demo by Phil Manzanera's Quiet Sun – was recorded in September 1970. The last – by Roxy Music themselves – was the UK number-4 hit 'Angel Eyes', released in August 1979. In between, both individually and collectively, Roxy Music set the pace not only for the decade itself, but also for those that followed.

For the vast majority of people who followed the band through those years, their introduction came that evening in August 1972 when Roxy Music made their debut on *Top of the Pops* – a shower of tinsel, glitter and quiffs, with Brian Eno in feathers and Bryan Ferry in leather, demanding 'What's her name? Virginia Plain?'

Even before *Top of the Pops,* however, a few late-night listeners had encountered Roxy Music, courtesy of three breathtaking John Peel sessions. A lucky handful had witnessed them live, begrudgingly paying their dues around the grubby clubs of the southeast. But it was the impact of television that introduced fame to Roxy Music – stylish, chic, utterly otherworldly, the best-dressed band in a year full of wondrous wardrobes.

Songs were word salads set to sci-fi soundtracks; the lyrics both aching with nostalgia and grasping the future. Solos were often savage and brief starbursts of sonics when you least expected them. And ringmaster of it all, Ferry – his very voice so immaculately styled that it was an instrument all of its own, its uniqueness rivalled only by the unfathomable banks of switches and wires over which Eno presided.

Across five albums, the moment you heard Roxy Music, you had to join in, if only to answer the questions with which their very existence peppered the pop scene. Can you do the strand? Does your dream home have a heartache? Are both ends still burning? From the moment that car door slams, love is still the drug.

Too much cheesecake too soon. Roxy Music broke up, then they made up, and between 1979 and 1982, the band unleashed three more albums – the distanced dance of *Manifesto,* which bade farewell to the 1970s, the skewered semi-soul of *Flesh And Blood*, and the lush soundscapes (but where's the song?) of *Avalon*. In other words, they simply carried on from exactly where they left off, and though the band's millennial reunion would not produce any new studio recordings, the live show (and accompanying CD and DVD) proved that the passage of time was one thing that Roxy Music need never fear. They were still the best thing on legs.

That was Roxy Music's secret – the fact that no one could doubt them, and none could outdo them: not Lou Reed, not T Rex. And as for David Bowie, well, as American impresario Jerry Brandt once quipped, he was tacky and he couldn't pirouette. Neither – it turned out – could Bryan Ferry. Rather, his favourite dance technique appeared to involve his abdomen remaining fixed into place while the rest of his body revolved slowly around it. In his case, however, it didn't matter. Why should it? Roxy may have sold us more gimmicks than Looney Tunes' ACME, but a blind man could see the difference. Art met artifice, and for the first time, no one lost.

So if you're there looking through that old picture frame, just waiting for the perfect view, let's go back to the day when something special walked into your life, and never walked out again.

1972 brought a lot of great bands to the fore, any one of whom in a normal year might have eclipsed all others in terms of sound and vision. That summer alone introduced *Top of the Pops* fans to Alice Cooper, David Bowie and Mott the Hoople, to join the Sweet, Slade and T. Rex in the glitter-ball stakes. But Roxy Music outstripped everyone, and continued to outstrip them for the remainder of the decade. And how? Because, in the end, they didn't merely shape the decade: in many ways, they *were* the decade.

Chapter One: Beginnings

There are two ways to tell the Roxy Music story. One is to delve into background and biography, to tell how Washington, County Durham-born Bryan Ferry was a Fine Arts student with a sideline in local bands The Banshees, The Gas Board and City Blues (none of which went anywhere); was a former schoolmaster teaching pottery to the youth of Holland Park; an aspiring singer who auditioned for King Crimson but didn't get the job; how he met former Westminster choirboy Andy Mackay through an ad Ferry placed in *Melody Maker*; how Mackay introduced Brian Eno to the mix (an aspiring avant-gardist whose inability to play any instrument had already seen him recruited to the Portsmouth Sinfonia): of whom, a lot more later); how drummer Paul Thompson came down from Newcastle with his own string of previous bands behind him (but at least he'd cut a record – the crunching blues of 'Got A Bad Leg' – with the wonderfully-named Smokestack Crumble), and so forth. That's one way of doing it.

The other is to follow the musical threads that led first to Roxy and then in a score of other directions, while focusing only on the core members of the band – those we have already met, of course, and the one we haven't: London-born, Cuba-raised guitarist Phil Manzanera.

Other members came and went. Former The Nice guitarist Davy O'List was an ultimately ill-fitting recruit in the band's early days. Ex-Curved Air keyboardist Eddie Jobson unenviably replaced Eno in the lineup, and saw out the end of Roxy's first era. And every time you turned around, they seemed to have another bassist: including past-and-future members of The Big 3, Quatermass, King Crimson, Family, Milk 'N' Cookies and Sparks. Each of these and more will come and go here, because nobody can deny that they were *in* Roxy Music. But they were never Roxy itself. In which case, the story begins…

September 1970: Quiet Sun – Demos

Personnel:
Phil Manzanera (aka Philip Targett-Adams): guitar
Charles Hayward: drums
Bill MacCormick: bass
Dave Jarrett: keyboards
Tracks: 'Trot', 'Years Of The Quiet Sun'*
Available on: The Manzanera Archives Rare One

Manzanera, Hayward and MacCormick had already been playing together as Pooh and the Ostrich Feather when in 1970, they were reborn as Quiet Sun: a band modelled almost wholly on their love for – and friendship with – Soft Machine. MacCormick's mother worked alongside Robert Wyatt's as a teaching assistant at Dulwich Prep, at a time when Wyatt and his fellow Softs were living on nearby Dalmore Street. The Softs were initially closest to MacCormick's older brother Ian (better-known as journalist/author Ian 'I. Mac' MacDonald), but the young Bill was also a regular visitor to the house: watching as Messrs. Wyatt, Hopper, Ratledge and Dean rehearsed in the front room, studiously oblivious to the complaints of the neighbours. Their influence quickly rubbed off.

Pooh and the Ostrich Feather (I. Mac coined the name) had started life as a covers band, honing their chops on Cream, Jefferson Airplane and a clutch of blues covers. They made their live debut with a three-song showcase at general arts show The Summer Miscellany, staged in Dulwich College's Great Hall, and the school remained their primary audience thereafter.

Slowly, however, they began to morph as Hayward and Manzanera began contributing their own compositions. The band's first original was the latter's 'Marcel My Dada'. MacCormick recalls:

Soft Machine had become the major influence in the '69-70 period, for no other reason than they were the band I knew personally and they were, pretty much, everyone's favourite at the time. Robert Wyatt was instrumental in broadening our musical tastes, especially on the jazz side, and my brother and I were lucky to have a very good music section on our local library. We had always listened to a lot of 19th-century music (Beethoven, Brahms, Tchaikovsky, etc.), and then my brother moved into Stravinsky, Prokofiev and Shostakovich. Then it was on to Berg, Messiaen, etc. Charles (Hayward) was also into the obscure and downright weird. When we started to rehearse at his parents' house in Camberwell, he would play us the newest stuff he had found, during our tea breaks: things like the United States of America's first album. We also got into world music: gamelan, Bulgarian folk singing, Indian music, etc.

By the time all three members were out of school (Manzanera and MacCormick left in 1969; Hayward the following year), Quiet Sun were almost wholly instrumental. 'It was during rehearsals at Phil's mum's place that I started to learn the bass parts', says MacCormick, 'otherwise we would have been unable to rehearse'. Unfortunately, they had to drop most of the vocals, because 'I could either play bass or sing, but not really both. I did do some singing on... demos, but it wasn't a strength'.

Advertisements in *Melody Maker* called for 'a keyboard player in the Ratledge style', a bass player and a sax player. Dave Jarrett was first to answer their call, followed by a former Army bandsman: saxman and flautist Dave Monaghan. MacCormick: 'Dave was quite a bit older than us, and though he played on the first demos we recorded, his need for money was too pressing and he had to get a paid gig somewhere. We sent out the demos as a five-piece, but carried on as a four-piece. Quiet Sun was the name arrived at under which the demos were sent to record companies, journalists, etc.'.

The band's first demo comprised two songs – Manzanera's 'Trot', and 'Years Of The Quiet Sun' written by McCormick and his brother, and developing into a ten-minute piece cut deep within Soft Machine territory – noodling keys, relentless bass, splashy percussion and Monaghan's melodic horns – all shot through with occasional (and already unmistakably Manzanera-shaped) guitar. It was, initially, a well-starred offering. *Melody Maker*'s Richard Williams was then authoring a column devoted to unknown bands' demo tapes, and Quiet Sun soon received their first-ever press mention. However, it was also their last: for now at least.

Already, Quiet Sun was operating on the very fringes of early-1970s prog, as Manzanera recalls: 'We spent much more time rehearsing than playing. We used to work up these amazing things and just practice them. It was very difficult to get gigs!'. Or to attract any further attention.

The labels to whom the tape had been sent, began responding. CBS turned the band down flat, and so did Liberty and Island. Indeed, the latter suggested 'Perhaps the guy who wrote the superb literate handout (that accompanied the tape) should stick to handouts ... I didn't think any of your music is that suitable for our label. Actually, I am not too knocked out with it, it seems to lack a lot of bite'. I. Mac – the author of that handout – certainly heeded that advice. The band members, however, were less prone to listen, because, amidst all the rejections, there came one ray of hope. Warner Brothers *were* impressed, and they wanted to hear more.

December 1970: The Portsmouth Sinfonia – Beethoven Today, Queen Elizabeth Hall, London

Personnel: Gavin Bryars, John Farley, Adrian Rifkin, James Lampard, Robin Mortimore, Brian Eno and others.

What became known as (but was never intended to be) the 'worst orchestra in the world' – The Portsmouth Sinfonia – was formed at Portsmouth Arts College in May 1970 as a one-off entrant in a spoof talent contest being organised by music teacher Gavin Bryars. The notion of an orchestra whose members needed to be either non-musicians or, if they could play something, take on an altogether different instrument, was not Bryars' alone. Fellow experimentalist Cornelius Cardew's similarly-inclined Scratch Orchestra got off the ground around a year earlier. As a short article in *Source* magazine (Issue 10) pointed out, however, the Sinfonia 'had nothing to do with ... the fringe of chaos (the Scratch Orchestra's stated destination); its members were interested in playing the popular classics to the best of their ability, without the gloss of technical expertise, but with a true enthusiasm for the enjoyment of their real entertainment value'. Neither was the talent show to be their sole adventure. So well-received was the Sinfonia's debut performance that they were soon plotting further shows. A flexi disc featuring that debut gig's version of the 'William Tell Overture' was distributed, and new blood was constantly offering to join the Sinfonia's ranks.

One such was an Ipswich-born student named Brian Eno. '(I'm) not sure exactly how I met Brian', Bryars mused, 'but he told me that he used to come to the concerts that John Tilbury and I did on the South Bank in 1969-71'. Now Eno was working for printmaker Ian Tyson, who handled many of Bryars' experimental scores, and when Bryars moved out of his small Kilburn flat for a new home in Ladbroke Grove, Eno moved in. By the time of the pre-Christmas *Beethoven Today*, he was the orchestra's clarinetist, adopting the instrument solely because his father could play it. Eno, on the other hand, couldn't. He, too, confirmed that any humour found in the Sinfonia's performances was not intentional. He told *Mojo* in 1995:

If there was a joke, it was always that much funnier when the people were trying to get it right: then the mistakes were very touching somehow. It never worked if people were trying to be funny. In fact, we chucked a guy out for farting around: a trumpet player who tried to make silly mistakes.

Being thrown out of the Portsmouth Sinfonia: that really must be the lowest of the low!

Journalist and composer Michael Nyman agreed, telling the *Sunday Times* about the first time he caught the Sinfonia in action: 'I sat through the first half, and I was so moved and entertained and excited by the music, that I went up to Gavin in the interval and said, 'Is there a spare instrument? I'd like to join'. They had a spare cello, so suddenly I was playing 'In The Hall Of The Mountain King' in the second half'.

But he, too, stressed, 'We were all serious artists or experimental musicians, and none of us actually joined to make funny music. Because of the skill structure of the Sinfonia, you couldn't fail to come up with outlandish results. But we weren't deliberately incompetent. And the combination of everybody's individual errors built a musical structure that was incomparable'.

Spring 1971: Quiet Sun – Warner Brothers demo
Personnel:
Phil Manzanera: guitar
Charles Hayward: drums
Bill MacCormick: bass
Dave Jarrett: keyboards
Tracks: 'Corazon Y Alma', 'RFD'
Both available on The Manzanera Archives Rare One

Quiet Sun recorded the Warners demo in the midst of the only concerted period of gigging they would ever undertake. Bill MacCormick recalls, 'We mainly played gigs in South London in local halls; some we self-promoted, perhaps a dozen. Our first-ever pro gig was very brief and pretty bad, and was on Worthing Pier, supporting Steamhammer. We also played a gig at St Dunstan's School in Catford, supporting Caravan. The important gig (for me) was at Portsmouth Polytechnic, where we supported Symbiosis, with Robert (Wyatt) on drums, and then jammed on stage with them later'.

Meanwhile, the Warners tape 'was recorded in an old mansion out in the Dorset countryside. The singing was done in the hallway and it was fun but incredibly rough and ready. Basically, we didn't know enough about recording, production etc. to make the most of it'. The two songs they recorded were now only a fraction of the repertoire. 'We had other material. I was writing, Charles had just finished 'Rongwrong', Dave was contributing'. Nevertheless, 'While we had improved dramatically live, the studio was still foreign territory'.

The band adapted well, regardless. Another ten-minute-plus epic, the raw but melodic 'Corazon Y Alma' is very much a Manzanera showcase, before a MacCormick vocal presses into view. 'RTD', on the other hand, lurches into full free-jazz territory: a rapid-fire conversation between bass, drums and piano, into which a hyperactive organ eventually inserts itself. Still, the overall impression was of music that was a lot more fun to play than to listen to, and when Warners rejected the tape, the end of Quiet Sun was inescapable. 'Both Phil and I had taken day jobs to keep the wolf from the door', says MacCormick. 'Then, in the early autumn, Phil answered the Roxy advert, and I was asked by Robert (Wyatt) to work on what became Matching Mole'.

Quiet Sun folded... quietly.

Early 1971: Smokestack Crumble – 'Got A Bad Leg' b/w 'Whisky Macaroni' (Single)

Personnel:
Dave McTavish: vocals
Paul Thompson: drums
Vic Malcolm: guitar
Produced by Keith Relf
Released 1971
Highest chart position: did not chart

Featuring former Tintern Abbey vocalist Dave McTavish and future Geordie guitarist Vic Malcolm alongside Paul Thompson, Smokestack Crumble were one of the more powerful bands signed to the Pye Records progressive subsidiary Dawn. They were also one of the shortest-lived. Produced by former Yardbirds frontman Keith Relf, their solitary single was a thunderous slab of blues rock, with a picture sleeve that offers collectors the first-published photograph of any future Roxy Music member. The record went nowhere, and the band followed. By the time Jarrow-born Thompson answered Roxy Music's latest drummer-wanted ad – as they sought a replacement for American Dexter Lloyd – he was working on a building site. 'He's very sensible and practical', Ferry told *Melody Maker* the following year; 'Getting up at seven o'clock in the morning and turning up for the gig in the evening still wearing his wellington boots...'.

The Smokestack Crumble experience was not wasted either. In September 1973, with Roxy Music searching for a new bass player, Thompson happened to walk into the Scene & Heard record shop on Tottenham Court Road, and who should be working behind the counter but Sal Maida: a New York bassist who he remembered from a Smokestack Crumble demo session. Weeks later, Maida would be on the road with Thompson.

DECADES | Roxy Music in the 70s

Chapter Two: Enter Roxy, Stage Left-field

May 1971: Roxy – Demos
Personnel:
Bryan Ferry: vocals, keyboards
Andy Mackay: sax
Roger Bunn: guitar
Graham Simpson: bass
Brian Eno: keyboards, electronics
Paul Thompson: drums
Tracks: 'Ladytron', '2 H.B.', 'Chance Meeting', 'The Bob (Medley)'
All available on: Roxy Music (Super Deluxe Edition)

Roxy (the 'Music' came a little later) had been around since the end of
1970, although Ferry later revealed it had been on his mind since 1964 or
so. He told the *New Musical Express*' John Ingham: 'The breakthrough, in
a way, was learning to play piano, because up to then I felt very frustrated.
I had things in my mind which I wanted to do, but I couldn't actually
play anything. I did play kind of mad piano, especially when drunk, but
then I started playing chords and worked on that for a year, and the songs
started coming out after that.'

The band had been led throughout by Ferry and bassist Simpson, an
old friend whose band Cock-a-Hoop had recently been lured south by
a management contract with Terry Ellis, only to break up soon after. 'I
looked him up, and for a time there was just two of us working, trying to
figure out where we could go from there. I had most of the songs then,
and I was playing piano, and Graham, bass ... the limitations of that lineup
are pretty obvious'.

Another Durham-days compatriot – Roger Bunn – moved in on
guitar, while ex-National Youth Orchestra horn player Mackay was next:
introduced by an artist friend after Ferry remarked that he was thinking
of buying a synthesizer. Mackay had one, and originally described himself
as a keyboard player only. But one day, he brought along an oboe, and on
another occasion, a saxophone, and there was no going back. Synth duties
were duly passed to his friend Eno. American-born Dexter Lloyd was the
band's original drummer but was replaced by Thompson in early-1971.

Roxy's first rehearsal room was in a derelict house in Kensington, and
they were still there a year later. As for the band's name, it came out
of a brainstorming session spent remembering the names of 1950s-era

cinemas. The Ritz, The Regal, The Granada... The Roxy!

Eno initially occupied an offstage role as the band's 'technical advisor': a job description that still enthuses his admirers. Echo and the Bunnymen's Will Sergeant recalled his first impressions of Eno for *Electronic Sound* magazine in 2021: '(He) wasn't a virtuoso. His job was making weird noises and fucking around with a tape recorder. And wearing feathers! Ha! Brilliant!'.

Richard H. Kirk of Cabaret Voltaire also spoke admiringly of Eno's example. He told author Simon Reynolds, 'Just listening to him [Eno] talk in interviews about how anyone can make music because you don't need to learn an instrument, you can make music with a tape recorder or a synth: that was the inspiration that really got us started'. The aspiring group was even happier when they discovered the university music department possessed the exact same kind of synth that Eno then employed.

At the time of his recruitment to Roxy, Eno had also become an occasional member of the Scratch Orchestra, and made his vinyl debut on their *The Great Learning* album, where he is credited with providing 'voice'. Any experiences gleaned from that venture however, were of no service at all as Roxy set to work on their first serious demo.

Looking back from 18 months later, Ferry was surprisingly open about the band's initial intentions: 'When we formed Roxy Music, we actually thought our music would be more experimental than it has been up to now', he told *Beat Instrumental*'s Steve Turner. 'I don't think Soft Machine were interesting enough. Pink Floyd were more interesting but still fell a little short. We're the most ideas-orientated band around'.

Phil Manzanera, who met the band a few months later, remembers, 'Their tape was done with a very abstract sort of classical drummer and all that sort of thing. It was very different'.

It drew attention, however. Reviewing the demo for *Melody Maker* in August 1971, Richard Williams described it as 'one of the most exciting tapes ever to come my way', and *that*, despite it having been recorded 'on a small home tape machine in what sounds like a Dutch barn'. He remarked on the unlikely nature of the band: 'Five years ago, it would have been unthinkable for Bryan Ferry to have entered rock and roll. Fine Arts graduates from Newcastle University just didn't do that sort of thing. But now, in 1971, Bryan is leading a band called Roxy (whose music) carries enough innovatory excitement to suggest that Roxy may well be ahead of the field in the avant-rock stakes'. Williams told Roxy's first-ever biographer – the late Johnny Rogan – that the tape was a mess:

'It sounded like people mucking around and there was this bloke in the middle who wanted to be a pop singer'.

Comparing the demo's contents with their eventual *finished* incarnations, the songs themselves are largely recognisable, at least in as much as lyric and melody are in place. It's the arrangements that astonish. 'Ladytron' is far more relaxed and considerably darker than any subsequent take, while '2 H.B.' – Ferry's ode to actor Humphrey Bogart – opens as a duet for tortured horn and martial timpani alone. Later, Bunn's guitar thunders against Ferry's vocal, while the stop/start arrangement and Mackay's gorgeous horn solo amidships have more in common with the as-yet-unwritten 'Sea Breezes' and 'If There Was Something' than the half-the-length version of '2 H.B.' that appeared on the band's first album – especially once the whole thing shatters into something approaching discordance before Ferry unleashes his full vocal range across a brief reprise of the song itself.

'Chance Meeting' would survive largely unchanged into the first LP sessions, barring the considerably eerier atmosphere that the band contrives behind the lyric. And 'The Bob (Medley)' – destined to become the most out-there track on the album – already feels fully formed: a fact that would be reinforced when Roxy were invited onto The John Peel Show five months after the *Melody Maker* review was published.

21 January 1972: Roxy Music – John Peel Show

All available on: Roxy Music (Super Deluxe Edition)
Personnel:
Bryan Ferry: vocals, keyboards
Andy Mackay: sax
Davy O'List: guitar
Brian Eno: vocals, keyboards, electronics
Graham Simpson: bass
Paul Thompson: drums
Produced by John Muir
Recorded Studio 1, Shepherd Bush, 4 January 1972
Tracks: 'Re-make/Re-model', 'The Bob (Medley)', 'Would You Believe?', 'If There Is Something', 'Sea Breezes'

The lineup had changed. Roger Bunn departed in the fall, and a *Melody Maker* ad recruited a string of hopefuls: among them, Phil Manzanera. He didn't get the job: 'I went along for an audition after seeing the ad in

Melody Maker, and I got on well with them, although they hated the tape I played to them. I auditioned and I didn't get the gig'.

Instead, Ferry approached former The Nice guitarist Davy O'List, himself at something of a loose end in the years since his departure from that band. 'By the time I joined', O'List says, 'Roxy Music had been rejected at least once by every record company in the land'.

Three of the songs from the May-1971 demo tape were reprised for the radio, and in every instance, all have edged much closer to their *finished* state: 'Re-make/Re-model' most noticeably. Where the demo began with drone and never perked up, now the staccato piano intro, the frenzied band assault and the closing bonsai solos, are all in place. Perhaps O'List can be accused of showboating a little… but why not? Besides, it's not as if he's alone in that – the entire band is going hell-for-leather, and if you never listened to another note from Roxy Music, this one performance would still be one of the most exciting things you've ever heard.

'Sea Breezes', however, is the *pièce de résistance* – the urgency in Ferry's vocal, the spectral moans of horn and guitar, the insistent wash of waves that underpin it all… and then an abrupt change: the military precision of the song's mid-section; O'List laying down some of his finest ever guitar lines. Small wonder that in the wake of the broadcast, Roxy's phone started ringing.

Live bookings followed. O'List recalls shows at Reading University's Fine Arts department and Battersea Art College, together with a handful of more mundane outings opening for Quintessence in Bristol and Cambridge. The most incongruous of them all, though, was with The Pretty Things in Aylesbury:

We were sitting in this freezing cold dressing room, while outside, the place was filling up with greasers. We just wanted to get the gig over with; we were expecting it to be really bad. In fact, we went down great. Bryan had made a quick quiff with a pot of Brylcreem, and there were all these greasers out there, actually jiving to the music! It was an amazing sight!

Listen to the Peel session take of 'Would You Believe?' and it is very easy to restage that memory in your own head; easy too to determine why Ferry later described this Peel session as one of the best Roxy recordings there is. Unfortunately, it would also be this lineup's last. Scant days later, at the end of January, Ferry was introduced to EG management by Robert Fripp, whom he met when auditioning for the vacant spot of Crimson vocalist the previous year. He was turned down with the suggestion that, with a voice and an approach like his, Ferry would be better off persevering with his own group.

EG was interested, but only in Ferry. A solo deal was offered, but the singer stuck to his guns. Finally, he convinced EG co-owner David Enthoven to accompany him to the Granada cinema on Wandsworth Road, south London, to see Roxy Music in action. Partner John Gaydon and journalist Richard Williams accompanied him.

Ferry knew what he was doing. 'You've got to use your intuition', he told Williams, 'We want to be with somebody civilised, and we don't want to make the mistake of signing something that we'll regret a couple of months later. There are so many things to take into consideration'. Bemused but impressed, and with Williams firmly on the band's side, EG agreed to take on the entire package. A week later, Roxy Music were signing to Island Records: one of the labels that had rejected them in the past. Davy O'List would not be joining them.

Phil Manzanera:

I used to bump into them in strange places, like a Steve Reich concert at the Queen Elizabeth Hall; they played the Friends Of The Tate Christmas party, and my friend was doing the lights, and in they all traipsed. I continued to be a friend; I was at their audition for EG, sitting with the two managers from EG, and Richard. But Davy was their guitarist. And then, during the audition, Davy had a punch-up with Paul Thompson, and that's when it was decided he had to go.

There was also a rumour going around that EG somehow engineered the split: anxious to keep O'List and Keith Emerson apart. The pair's shared past in The Nice had not ended at all pleasantly. O'List subsequently denied this.

Meanwhile, Manzanera had not been idle: 'They asked me to audition again, and by that time, I'd secretly learned all their material, sussed out what they wanted to do. I didn't tell them this, of course; didn't tell them for a long time, but I played and they thought, 'Christ, he must be a genius!'.

6 June 1972: Roxy Music – Royal College of Art
Personnel:
Bryan Ferry: vocals, keyboards

Andy Mackay: sax
Phil Manzanera: guitar
Rick Kenton: bass
Brian Eno: keyboards, electronics
Paul Thompson: drums
Track: 'Re-make/Re-model'

Our earliest-surviving glimpse of Roxy Music in person is this specially-shot Island Records promo capturing the band in performance and has as keen an eye for video trickery as for the musicians themselves. No matter. Lit by Dave Horsefield, directed by the London-based Visualeyes Ltd. and edited by Doug Smith, the excitement is palpable, the costumes kaleidoscopic, and so enticing was the imagery that when Virgin Records (owners of the Roxy catalogue during the 1980s) came to compile the *Street Life: 20 Great Hits* collection, a still from the video was selected for the cover. The full footage appears on the super deluxe edition of *Roxy Music.*

20 June 1972: Roxy Music – The Old Grey Whistle Test (TV)

Personnel:
Bryan Ferry: vocals, keyboards
Andy Mackay: sax
Phil Manzanera: guitar
Rick Kenton: bass
Brian Eno: keyboards, electronics
Paul Thompson: drums
Tracks: 'Re-make/Re-model', 'Ladytron'

Early rumblings from the UK media were not welcoming. Journalists still expected bands to have paid their dues, and drummer Thompson aside, not one of them could be said to have done so – not jazz rocker Manzanera with his handful of support gigs; not Ferry, with his background in forgotten provincial club bands, and certainly not non-musician Eno. Rather, the handful of live performances that Roxy could point to, had gifted them with a following far removed from the hairy hordes that the music press admired: avant-garde student types, fashion designers, models, artists.

In the age of the Bolan boogie and the Zeppelin stomp, what could Roxy Music possibly have to offer? *Gimmicky*, screamed the band's greatest foes, their eyes landing like lasers on the hapless Eno. For, not only did he not play an instrument, it was his fault that nobody else's instrument sounded like it ought to: as Manzanera explained to *Trouser Press* a decade later: 'My guitar was patched into Eno's VCS3 (a modular synthesizer made by EMS) and through a couple of Revoxs (tape recorders) as synthesizers and all the new pedals, guitarists can do for themselves (what Eno did in Roxy Music). If Roxy Music were starting now (1982), perhaps we'd all be playing keyboards'.

The disdain was contagious. When Roxy Music made their debut on *The Old Grey Whistle Test* (20 June 1972) performing 'Re-make/Re-model' and a 'Ladytron' that did not so much end, as leap screaming off a cliff, host Bob Harris informed the watching millions that the group had been booked wholly against his wishes. ('Ladytron' appears on the super deluxe edition of *Roxy Music.*) They were, in his opinion, simply a talentless hype, just one more in the burgeoning production line of so-called glam rockers that had arisen in Marc Bolan's spangled wake. Even worse, Bryan Ferry did not seem to disagree. He told *Beat Instrumental*: 'I can see why the (glam) thing has come about. It's a reaction against what was going on onstage before. The performers were no different from the audience. I've always thought that if you're going to present yourself on stage, you should dress up. Even with my college band Gas Board, we wore bobby-sox suits with our initials on the pockets!'. It was, however, 'rather sad for us. The layman can't tell the difference between Gary Glitter and Roxy Music!'.

Yet, appearing at the Great Western Express Pop Festival in Lincoln on 27 May, Roxy Music were the stars of the show, and it was around this time that Bill MacCormick *almost* joined the band. He recalls:

Graham Simpson, the bass player, had a breakdown just before they were due to play (at Lincoln – Simpson's final show with Roxy was at Bristol University on 3 March). I was called but (Matching Mole) were off to Paris, and so Rick Kenton (ex-Woody Kern) did the gig and carried on for a while. When he left, they did look for someone, and I talked it over with Phil, but he told me they were really looking for a particular player, and if he was available, then no one else would be considered. He was and I wasn't. I doubt I would have fitted in anyway. Disciplined bass parts were not my thing at the time.

From hereon in, Roxy Music would remain on the road almost solidly until mid-August, with the nature of the venues they played tracing the solidly-upward trajectory that their career was now following.

28 May 1972 (unknown venue) Southsea
31 May 1972 Marquee Club, London
04 June 1972 Jazz Club, Redcar
05 June 1972 (unknown venue) Chester
10 June 1972 Floral Hall, Hornsea
14 June 1972 Stadium, Liverpool
15 June 1972 South Bank Polytechnic, London
16 June 1972 Van Dyke, Plymouth
21 June 1972 Sheffield University, Sheffield
24 June 1972 University of East Anglia, Norwich
25 June 1972 Croydon Greyhound, London
27 June 1972 Walbrook College, London
29 June 1972 Lancaster University
30 June 1972 Empire Pool Wembley London (opening for Alice Cooper)
01 July 1972 (unknown venue) Halifax
02 July 1972 New Theatre, Oxford
04 July 1972 (unknown venue) Wood Green, London
07 July 1972 Red Lion, Leytonstone
08 July 1972 (unknown venue) Chippenham
09 July 1972 Locarno, Bristol (opening for Hawkwind)
14 July 1972 City Hall, Salisbury
15 July 1972 Memorial Hall, Northwich
22 July 1972 Civic Hall, Dunstable
23 July 1972 Black Prince, Bexley
25 July 1972 Grammar School, Hornchurch
26 July 1972 St Georges Hall, Liverpool
27 July 1972 Kensington Court Club, London
28 July 1972 Harrow Inn, Abbey Wood
29 July 1972 Crystal Palace Garden Party Festival, London
31 July 1972 George Hotel, Stoke on Trent
05 August 1972 Friars, Aylesbury
06 August 1972 Chelsea Village, London

23 June 1972: Roxy Music – John Peel Show

Tracks: 'Bitter's End', '2 H.B.'*, 'Chance Meeting'*, 'Ladytron'*
*available on Roxy Music (Super Deluxe Edition)
Personnel:

Bryan Ferry: vocals, keyboards
Andy Mackay: sax
Phil Manzanera: guitar
Peter Paul: bass (Named in the BBC's session documents. Other sources credit Rik Kenton.)
Brian Eno: keyboards, electronics
Paul Thompson: drums
Produced by John Muir.
Recorded Studio 1, Shepherds Bush, 23 May 1972.

By May, Roxy Music were in the studio recording their debut album with producer Pete Sinfield. (An album's worth of outtakes from the sessions appear on the super deluxe edition.) It was a fascinating combination. Like Eno with Roxy Music, Sinfield had once very much been an offstage contributor to King Crimson's onstage activities, and – again, like Eno – those contributions were enormous. Sinfield is best recalled as Crimson's primary lyricist, but it would not be stretching credulity to argue that Eno's electronics seasoned Roxy's music as much as Sinfield's words flavoured Crimson's. It's also worth noting another prevalent rumour – that the main reason Eno was shifted from his accustomed roost in the auditorium, was because EG didn't want to have to deal with another offstage band member.

It was a shame, though. As Ferry told *Beat Instrumental*, those early gigs were 'a scream ... Eno would be talking to a member of the audience, you know, telling him what kind of a PA and mixer we were using, and then he'd have to break off and sing a few harmonies into the desk mic, which would then come out from on stage'.

Swathes of the album were already in the can by the time Roxy filed into the BBC's Studio T1 at Kensington House to record another Peel session. Perhaps dulled by the musicians' own familiarity with the songs, the result is the least dramatic of all Roxy's early broadcasts.

Chapter Three: The Answer to a Maiden's Prayer

June 1972: Roxy Music – Roxy Music (LP)

Personnel:
Bryan Ferry: vocals, keyboards
Andy Mackay: sax
Phil Manzanera: guitar
Graham Simpson: bass
Brian Eno: keyboards, electronics
Paul Thompson: drums
Produced by Pete Sinfield
Recorded Command Studios, London, 14-29 March 1972
Release date 16 June 1972
Highest chart positions: UK: 10, US: did not chart
Tracks: 'Re-make/Remodel', 'Ladytron', 'If There Is Something', '2 H.B.', 'The Bob (Medley)', 'Chance Meeting', 'Would You Believe?', 'Sea Breezes', 'Bitter End (US pressings include 'Virginia Plain')

The band did not initially rate their chances of mainstream success too highly. As Ferry told *The Guardian* in 2018, they assumed their audience would be 'art students; people like us; limited interest; underground. Coming overground was… interesting'. The uncertainty was understandable. Again in that *Guardian* piece, he reflected:

> The clothes we were wearing at that time would have put off quite a large chunk of people. What I liked about the American bands, the Stax label and Motown, they were into presentation and show business; mohair suits, quite slick. And the cover art, I thought of all the American pop culture icons, Marilyn Monroe: selling cigarettes or beer with a glamorous image. But it was a bit off-kilter as well – there was something a bit strange about it, futuristic as well as retro. All that – instead of a picture of the band – in a dreary street, looking rather sullen, which was the norm.

Maybe it was that refusal to follow leaders that did the trick. Roxy Music's eponymous debut album certainly cut through all the media uncertainty – the most often-quoted review is the *New Musical Express* offering that declares the album to be 'the answer to a maiden's prayer', but such praise was scarcely alone. Reliably, Richard Williams (*Melody Maker*) feted 'an extraordinary album, from an extraordinary group'. I. Mac (again, not surprisingly) gave over his next *New Musical Express* spread to, effectively, Ferry's manifesto for success. But elsewhere too, the press flocked to Roy's banner, and while I. Mac acknowledged 'Much play was made at the time of the album's release, of the weird mixture of styles in Roxy's music', that was scarcely a bad thing.

The Times got in on the action, indicating just how quickly Roxy had risen, by reviewing *Roxy Music* alongside new albums by T. Rex, Rod Stewart and David Bowie: the latter of whom Richard Williams (again!) remarked was not as bright as Bryan Ferry. Or rather, he was, but Ferry 'puts his brain and his modish eclecticism to better use, on the band's brilliant debut album. In no time at all, Roxy has become the most talked-about group in the country, and the album provides most of the reasons. They use electronics, but sparingly, and the album is strong on unusual textures and apt production devices. Like Bowie, they wear sparkly fancy dress on stage, but they have more depth – more power in reserve – than he'.

Even Simon Frith, isolating what he felt was one of the album's biggest faults for *Let It Rock,* did so in such a way that it also sounds like an advantage:

> Roxy Music could easily be as cold and calculated as Bryan Ferry sometimes seems to hope... Camp, it could be. Take all of rock's well-oiled forms, hand 'em high and milk the message out of them. I think the first Roxy album... has just this failing. Bitty, jokey, endless empty references, gimmicky production, clever and uncertain. It all seemed kinda pointless... A *knowing* record.

Yes, and that was part of its appeal. As Ferry remarks at the conclusion of 'Bitter's End': 'Note his reaction acid sharp should make the cognoscenti think'. Fabulous. It'll do them good.

Roxy Music was also wholly purposeful. As Ferry remarked – again to I. Mac – 'What interests me, far more than ambiguity, is juxtaposing things, so they shock. I like surprise'.

Roxy Music was a surprise.

It begins on the bus ride home. The album's out of its bag, and model Kari-Ann Muller is draped across a gatefold outer, and only Kari-Ann. It was a startling image. In any other circumstances, it would be cheesecake pure and simple. But in Roxy Music's hands, it was an invitation. It would be close to 40 years before the super-deluxe edition informed us that the chosen cover was just one of dozens of photographs shot by Karl Stoeker and styled by Anthony Price that afternoon. Dozens! Some in white, some in lime, but all of them sublime. But deceptive too. Although the band's name is writ large enough, this could still be an ad for a box of especially high-end chocolates, and you need to open the gatefold to find pictures of the musicians themselves: head and shoulders-plus, glammed to the nines, but beyond glam too. Even the liner notes by press man Simon Puxley seemed otherworldly – laying out in blue on silver precisely what you should expect from the music, until the slow crawl of the number 11 bus felt more interminable than ever.

You'd never have guessed that just three songs in, Bryan Ferry would be dreaming of growing potatoes.

The reviews dug deep in search of conceivable influences; sundry writers suggesting actor Humphrey Bogart (for obvious reasons) and singer Ethel Merman; doo-wop and old rockers; sea breezes and crowded parties. And that in itself is a more varied palette than most. Where Roxy excelled was in so effortlessly melding them, that no sound, no influence, was more pronounced than any other, and the nine individual songs that comprised *Roxy Music* might have offered any other band, nine entire LPs.

For the select handful who had followed Roxy through the year – from the earliest shows and across the Peel broadcasts – little about *Roxy Music* could be called a surprise: indeed, those two sessions had already previewed the record's entire contents. But even for them, the finished item was indeed *finished*. Could Paul Thompson have ever improved on the beatless beat that drives the second half of 'Sea Breezes'? Could Ferry have put more passion into the *Casablanca* quotes of '2 H.B.'? Could the entire lineup have devised more perfect mini-solos for the close of 'Re-make/Re-model'? The answers are almost unfailingly 'No'. Ferry himself revisited all three as B-sides during his early solo career, and in each instance, they are covers in every sense of the word – to join Mike McGear's version of 'Sea Breezes', which even brother Paul McCartney could not stretch beyond its blueprint; Andy Mackay revisiting 'Bitter's End', and most grisly of all, Tin Machine's 'If There is Something'. Because, if you thought Bryan Ferry made an unlikely spud farmer, imagine *Bowie* out there in his wellies and cap.

August 1972: Roxy Music – 'Virginia Plain' b/w 'The Numberer' (Single)

Personnel:
Bryan Ferry: vocals, keyboards

Andy Mackay: sax
Phil Manzanera: guitar
Rik Kenton: bass
Brian Eno: keyboards, electronics
Paul Thompson: drums
Produced by Pete Sinfield
Recorded Command Studios, London, 10-12 July 1972
Release date 4 August 1972
Highest chart positions: UK: 4, US: did not chart

Island Records hoped Roxy would release 'Re-make/Re-model' as their debut single, and other voices apparently agreed. The band, however, already knew what their first 45 would be. Ferry told *I. Mac*, 'I thought it was a better move to release 'Virginia Plain' rather than something from the album'. He also mused aloud of including 'another rougher version of it on the next album, or a live cut on the B-side of a single, though I'm not really in favour of things like that'. It was not an easy record to perfect. Ferry continued: 'The first mix was nice and rough and had a lot of life in it, though the motorbike wasn't on it; then we did another one which I thought was too refined? And finally – because it was a rush release – Peter (Sinfield) had to do a third mix somewhere in between without us there. But I like it'.

'Virginia Plain' took its title and elements of its lyric from a painting Ferry executed during his art school days in Newcastle eight years previously: a giant pack of cigarettes with a picture of Warhol superstar Baby Jane Holzer on the front. The lyric itself was scattershot, myriad in-jokes and casual references that opened with a plea to the band's solicitor ('Make me a deal…') before embarking upon a wild drive through the American West and beyond. 'The song came together quickly', recalls Manzanera: 'We started with chords, no top-lines or anything. Bryan wrote the top line without anybody having any idea what the song was about'. He also admits that he has never been able to duplicate the solo, which explodes from the middle of the song: 'I just went *Blam!*.

But it was that seemingly-on-the-fly presentation that truly made the record both visual (that *Top of the Pops* performance) and aural. There was the 16-second intro that gave you no clue what was going to happen next, and a song that both started and finished so peremptorily that you were still waiting for the next verse long after the final word echoed to a halt.

First impressions are important, and that's basically what 'Virginia Plain' was: one first impression after another – the instrumental break that tinkled and crashed, and then that fabulous moment when the last verse breaks so triumphantly back in, only to slam to a halt 21 seconds later. All were tricks that the band had perfected across the LP, but none were familiar to the average teenage pop picker. 'Virginia Plain' was a record like no other.

Flip the single, and the first in what became a Roxy tradition of non-album B-sides, fuzzes into view – a duet for sax and synth that could as easily have spun out of a jam as be the fruits of a serious recording session but was all the more captivating for it. In common with Roxy Music's other early B-sides, 'The Numberer' would not be collected onto a long-player until 1995's *The Thrill Of It All* box set. 'Virginia Plain', despite its absence from the UK *Roxy Music* album, would be added to the American version.

1 August 1972: Roxy Music – John Peel Show (BBC Radio)

Personnel:
Bryan Ferry: vocals, keyboards
Andy Mackay: sax
Phil Manzanera: guitar
Rik Kenton: bass
Brian Eno: keyboards, electronics
Paul Thompson: drums
Produced by Pete Ritzema, Mike Franks.
Recorded Studio 4, Maida Vale, 18 July 1972
Tracks: 'Virginia Plain'*, 'If There Is Something'
*Available on Roxy Music (Super Deluxe Edition)

Past Roxy radio sessions showcased the songs and the musicianship. This time, it was the vision that was on display, as a career-best 'If There Is Something' devoured all but a hit's single span of the session: a duet for Mackay and Manzanera in and around one of Ferry's most laconic lyrics. Indeed, this particular take of 'If There Is Something' remains among the most essential performances in the entire Roxy Music canon – a near-12-minute showcase of everything for which Roxy would become renowned, and for a few things that they lost along the way: including that heart-stopping moment precisely at the seven-minute mark when everything suddenly halts, but only for a moment.

Ferry's voice strays fearlessly in directions he would never dare walk again, and never more so than during the song's nostalgia-steeped coda: 'Shake your hair girl, with that pony tail/Takes me right back…'. And he's almost wailing his distress because he knows he's correct, or at least that he *will* be. The trees were indeed taller, the grass was far greener, and the heels really *were* a great deal higher when you were young.

The performance's absence from any official release (including the BBC disc in the first album's super-deluxe edition) is among the most convincing arguments for the existence of bootlegs that has ever been conceived.

19-20 August 1972: Roxy Music – Rainbow Theatre, London

Personnel:
Bryan Ferry: vocals, keyboards
Andy Mackay: sax
Phil Manzanera: guitar
Rik Kenton: bass
Brian Eno: keyboards, electronics
Paul Thompson: drums
Tracks: 'Virginia Plain', 'The BOB (Medley)', '2 H.B.', 'Would You Believe?', 'Sea Breezes', 'Ladytron', 'If There Is Something', 'Re-make/Re-model'

So quickly did 'Virginia Plain' hit the chart, and so high did it climb once it got there (number 4), that by the time Roxy Music opened for David Bowie at The Rainbow, it was difficult to say who best deserved top billing. It would be Christmas before Bowie enjoyed a bigger hit ('Jean Genie') than Roxy scored with their very first try.

Roxy were late additions to the Rainbow bill, being added – it was said – at the headliner's own request. He was certainly enamoured with them – 18 months later, with Bowie recording his *Pin Ups* album in France, visiting journalist Charles Shaar Murray spotted the sheet music for 'Ladytron' lying around the studio. It was Murray who reviewed the Rainbow show:

Roxy Music proved that they are now in a major band not just in the eyes of publicists, friends and a few partisan journalists, but to audiences as well. Starting out with their glitzy teenage hit single 'Virginia Plain', they played a tight, neat set of songs from their spiffy first album. Each number earned a successively-warmer response, and Phil Manzanera's guitar temper tantrum went down especially well. They closed with 'Re-make/Re-model' and went off to a standing ovation.... Onwards and upwards, and here's looking at you, kid.

Both of Roxy's shows were preserved on handheld cassette recorders, from out in the audience someplace. And as such, they are a challenging listen for all but the most dedicated ears. Persevere, however, and the first night's rendition of 'If There Is Something' sounds like it could have been as good as any, and the drum roll with which Thompson introduces the second night's 'Would You Believe?' pumped adrenalin into the very back of the stalls.

'Ladytron' too packs dramatic energy, and it seems incredible that the earliest readily-available live recording of Roxy Music should also be one of the last at which their debut album dominated the set. By the time the microphones rolled for their BBC *In Concert* broadcast a month later, material destined for the new album was already leaking into the repertoire.

24 August 1972: Roxy Music – Top of the Pops (TV)
26 August 1972: The Portsmouth Sinfonia – International Carnival of Electronic Sound (ICES), Roundhouse, London.

Two days after Roxy Music's epochal appearance on *Top of the Pops* (The footage appears on the super-deluxe edition of *Roxy Music*), Eno was onstage again, this time as The Portsmouth Sinfonia closed the final night of the two-week festival of the avant-garde, ICES. But if anybody in the audience recognised the ensemble's clarinettist, they didn't say (or shout out) anything.

The orchestra appeared before an appreciative audience: the '1812 Overture' raised a laugh before the musicians had even started playing. A couple of selections from the soundtrack to *2001: A Space Odyssey*, rolled haplessly into the crosshairs, and they finished with an exquisite 'In The Hall Of The Mountain King'.

'They do something that could only happen (and flourish, perhaps) in England', wrote author Gordon Mumma, covering the festival for *Source* magazine. 'And the result is so beautiful that I must beg the inability to describe it'.

A 26-minute recording of the performance was broadcast by organiser Harvey Matusow on KPFA radio the following August during an interview with Charles Amirkhanian. But in common with the vast majority of the ICES festival, no official release has ever been forthcoming.

16 September 1972: Roxy Music – In Concert (BBC Radio)

Personnel:
Bryan Ferry: vocals, keyboards
Andy Mackay: sax
Phil Manzanera: guitar
Rik Kenton: bass
Brian Eno: keyboards, electronics
Paul Thompson: drums
Tracks: 'The Bob (Medley)'*, 'The Bogus Man Part 2 (Grey Lagoons)', 'Sea Breezes'*, 'Virginia Plain'*, 'Chance Meeting'*,'Re-make'/'Re-model'*
*Available on Roxy Music (Super Deluxe Edition)

It was a vivid performance, but do spare a thought for the hapless host Bob Harris. Scant months after bemoaning Roxy Music's appearance on *The Old Grey Whistle Test*, tonight he's telling us how much he'd been looking forward to seeing them. The band reward his newfound munificence with both a powerful performance and a first-broadcast airing for a song so new that they still referred to it under its working title 'The Bogus Man (Part 2)'. Clearly, the band's next album was stirring.

This broadcast would not receive an official release until the first album's super-deluxe edition (and even there, it lacks the new song). Until then, the bootleg *Better Than Food* kept it in circulation.

Opening for Roxy Music on the show was the folk duo Tír na nÓg, whose own performance that night was released in 2021 as the slightly mistitled *Live 1970-'71*. 'The crowd would not stop clapping for us', singer Leo O'Kelly recalled for the album's liner notes. 'The producer was doing his nut, as were Roxy, who were waiting in the wings. I'm sure someone would have thought we had plants in the audience, except we'd been booked at the last minute as a replacement for Gallagher and Lyle, who couldn't do it due to illness. Anyway, it was embarrassing... in the nicest possible way!'.

Chapter Four: Stay Cool is the Main Rule

9 November 1972: Roxy Music – John Peel Show

Personnel:

Bryan Ferry: vocals, keyboards

Andy Mackay: sax

Phil Manzanera: guitar

Rick Kenton: bass

Brian Eno: keyboards, electronics

Paul Thompson: drums

Tracks: 'The Bob (Medley)', 'For Your Pleasure', 'The Bogus Man'

Produced by Bernie Andrews

Recorded Langham I, 6 November 1972

Bryan Ferry devoted much of the summer to promoting Roxy Music, moving house and having his tonsils removed. He had barely recovered from that when Roxy's schedule for the remainder of the year was unveiled:

19 October 1972 Queens Hall, Leeds

24 October 1972 Tricorn Centre, Portsmouth

29 October 1972 (unknown venue) Weston-Super-Mare

30 October 1972 (unknown venue) Reading

31 October 1972 (unknown venue) Chatham

03 November 1972 Lanchester College, Rugby

04 November 1972 (unknown venue) Coventry

05 November 1972 Top Rank, Birmingham

08 November 1972 Liverpool Stadium, Liverpool

09 November 1972 Hardrock, Manchester

10 November 1972 Sheffield University, Sheffield

11 November 1972 City Hall, Newcastle

12 November 1972 (unknown venue) Redcar

17 November 1972 Trent Polytechnic, Nottingham

18 November 1972 Leicester University

19 November 1972 Greyhound, Croydon

20 November 1972 (unknown venue) Guildford

22 November 1972 University of York

23 November 1972 Victoria Hall Hanley

24 November 1972 Lancaster University, Lancaster

26 November 1972 Bataclan, Paris, France

What Ferry really wanted to do – needed to be doing – was writing more songs. *Roxy Music* was the product of two years of writing and revising, honing and shifting. Now the songbook was all but empty, and it showed. The one circulating live recording from this period – a challenging murky tape of the Guildford gig on 20 November – suggests none of the new songs felt likely to displace the best (read, 'all') of their debut album.

Nevertheless, two new numbers were deemed fit for broadcast radio, as the band returned to John Peel once again: 'The Bogus Man' and 'For Your Pleasure'. The full Peel session does not circulate. What we do have is an incomplete blast of what sounds like a truly incendiary 'The Bob', and a very rudimentary 'For Your Pleasure', initially delivered in the closest Ferry has ever come to a falsetto. Beyond that, the performance simply goes nowhere, preferring to plod half-heartedly along with only Manzanera's ghostly guitar for company. It also takes so long to fade out (close to three minutes), that it's maybe not surprising that the original taper seems to have lost interest when it finished.

Though the entirety of this session is lost, two other band appearances from this period are at least partially available. From the 25 November edition of the BBC's *Full House,* a still-tentative 'For Your Pleasure' appears on the *The Thrill Of It* All DVD video collection, while a strangely sparse and eerily *Enossified* 'Ladytron' and an oddly truncated 'Re-make/Re-model' can be found on the super-deluxe edition of *Roxy Music. (*A rambunctious 'The Bogus Man (Part Two)' remains unavailable.)

The super-deluxe also features four cuts from French TV's broadcast of the Paris Bataclan concert on 26 November, although this latter is something of a curate's egg. The sound quality is rough, with way too much distortion and drama around Ferry's vocals, and – for the first time in the band's television history – the camerawork simply isn't up to the band's costumery, while the musicians themselves are considerably more static than in other footage of the period. An oddly tedious 'Would You Believe?', opens, before a disappointingly edited 'If There Is Something' clips both the song's opening moments and a sizeable portion of the instrumental break and closing choruses. An atmospheric 'Sea Breezes' makes up for some of the disappointment, though, and – at last – a hyperactive 'Virginia Plain' completes the show. But as a showcase for what was now being touted as being among the most exciting bands of the age, it was a remarkably downbeat performance. One also forgets just how restrictive Ferry's piano-playing duties were at the time: how can you do the strand when you're nailed to a baby grand?

Meanwhile, a fourth new song – 'Beauty Queen' – was also apparently heading towards its unveiling when Ferry revealed it was under consideration as Roxy Music's next single: 'We're not a singles group really', he told I. Mac in the *New Musical Express* in October. 'I certainly don't want to find myself sliding down that Slade/T. Rex corridor of horror. We might release another one at Christmas, providing we've got strong-enough material. I've got some numbers in the pipeline, and one of them might well make a good single eventually. It's a ballad called 'Beauty Queen', and will be grandiose and heavy in the Walker Brothers tradition'.

The question was, would they even have a chance to record it? No, they wouldn't. Little more than a week after the Bataclan show, Roxy Music set off to discover America. They would even be spending Christmas there.

07 December 1972 Ohio University, Athens, OH
08 December 1972 Madison Square Garden, New York, NY
09 December 1972 Soldiers And Sailors Memorial Auditorium, Chattanooga, TN
10 December 1972 Civic Center, Charleston, WV
11 December 1972 Bijoux Club, Philadelphia PA
12 December 1972 Cobo Hall, Detroit, MI
13 December 1972 Hollywood Palladium, Los Angeles, CA
14 December 1972 (unknown venue) Los Angeles, CA
15 December1972 Selland Arena, Fresno, CA
16 December 1972 Civic Auditorium, Bakersfield, CA
19 December 1972 Whisky a Go Go, Los Angeles, CA
20-21 December 1972 Milwaukee Club, Milwaukee, WI
22-23 December 1972 Winterland, San Francisco, CA
26 December 1972 Curtis Hixon Hall, Tampa, FL
27 December 1972 Miami Speedway, Miami, FL
28 December 1972 Coliseum, Charlotte, NC
29 December 1972 Cumberland County Auditorium, Fayetteville, NC
30 December 1972 (unknown venue) Augusta, GA
31 December 1972 Kinetic Playground, Chicago, IL
02-04 January 1973 My Mother's Place, Washington,

America hated them. Audiences hated them. Critics hated them. By the time the tour was over, even Roxy Music hated them. Uncomprehending audiences, a 25-minute set limit and inappropriate headline acts were not a cocktail that showed any group in their best light, and every passing performance only added to the misery of Roxy Music's predicament: 'Every band we played with, we were totally bored by', Ferry sighed. 'Edgar Winter, Humble Pie, Jethro Tull, Jo Jo Gunne. All boring'.

'The first American tour was a terrible bringdown really', Ferry told *Melody Maker*'s Chris Charlesworth a couple of years later. 'It was the only time we've ever been... er, not appreciated. It was sandwiched between two English tours which were rave tours, and to come here and be totally unknown was obviously a bit of a downer. People I spoke to on that tour who had the first album never even knew we were due to play in the town on that day'.

If audiences were apathetic, the critics could be downright hostile: both at the time and later. *Creem*'s Robot A. Hull devoted much of his *For Your Pleasure* review to denouncing the band's onstage image, and admitted that if Roxy had a TV show, they'd probably break through big time: 'But it'll never happen. These guys are much too hot for all that. They got an ample supply of too much of nothing going for 'em. Give this album two months, and I betcha you'll be able to find it for 99 cents at your local Kmart'.

Eno alone admitted to having fun, and that turned out to be a mistake, if not a fully-fledged cardinal sin. Cautiously discussing a growing breach between himself and Ferry, Eno sighed, 'I actually enjoyed myself in America, which didn't help'.

March 1973: Roxy Music – 'Pyjamarama' b/w 'The Pride And The Pain' (Single)
Personnel:
Bryan Ferry: vocals, keyboards
Andy Mackay: sax
Phil Manzanera: guitar
John Porter: bass
Brian Eno: keyboards, electronics
Paul Thompson: drums
Produced by Chris Thomas, John Anthony, Roxy Music
Recorded AIR Studios, February 1973
Release date 23 February 1973
Highest chart positions: UK: 10, US: did not chart

Home from the US, bassist Kenton left the band to embark upon a sporadic solo career, highlighted by two 45s – the adorably breathy reggae bop of 'Bungalow Love' (still under the aegis of both Island Records and EG Management) in 1974, and 'The Libertine' in 1976. He later reappeared in the 1980s band Savage Progress.

Meanwhile, Roxy Music reached out to bassist John Porter: another of Ferry's bandmates from the days of The Gas Board. And though it had taken them seven months, they finally released a follow-up to 'Virginia Plain': a not altogether dissimilar blast of sound built around a paean to a woman with whom – or so Ferry suggests – he'd like to 'bill and coo'. A rush of adrenaline-fuelled excitement at the time, 'Pyjamarama' has since been revealed as probably the weakest of all Roxy's 1972-1975 singles. It still reached number 10 in the UK, but some choice lyrics aside, it really doesn't do much of anything. In fact, in the United States, 'Pyjamarama' would be overlooked altogether as a single in favour of 'Do The Strand'.

More intriguing is Andy Mackay's B-side – an arctic blast of crunching footsteps and howling wind that left one wondering just how exhilarating a vocal-less, Ferry-free Roxy might've sounded. Mackay, incidentally, would end the year as something of a top-30 veteran. Having already guested on Mott the Hoople's late-1972 'Honaloochie Boogie' hit, he was recalled for its follow-up 'All The Way From Memphis'.

28 February 1973 (recording date. Broadcast date unknown): Roxy Music – Network Session (BBC Radio)

Personnel:
Bryan Ferry: vocals, keyboards
Andy Mackay: sax
Phil Manzanera: guitar
John Porter: bass
Brian Eno: keyboards, electronics
Paul Thompson: drums
Tracks: 'Pyjamarama'
Produced by Pat Whelan
Recorded Playhouse Theatre, Northumberland Avenue, 28 February 18973

8 March 1973 Roxy Music – John Peel Show

Personnel:
Bryan Ferry: vocals, keyboards
Andy Mackay: sax
Phil Manzanera: guitar
Sal Maida: bass
Brian Eno: keyboards, electronics

Paul Thompson: drums
Produced by Bernie Andrews
Recorded Langham 1, 5 March 1973
Tracks: 'Editions Of You', 'Pyjamarama', 'In Every Dream Home A Heartache'

'Pyjamarama' may or may not have received its broadcast premier on a
BBC Radio *Network Session* on 28 February. According to BBC historian
Ken Garner's *In Session Tonight*, some uncertainty surrounds the
broadcast, if not the very recording of the performance.

The Peel outing, however, circulates in underground circles, and
skipping past a perfunctory rendition of the single, rejoices instead in two
distinct faces of the upcoming new album. 'Editions Of You' is breakneck
verbiage topped by some of Ferry's most timely one-liners ('Old money's
better than new' - Britain had adopted decimal coinage just two years
earlier), and delivered with a far sharper edge than the album cut would
be; 'In Every Dream Home', contrarily, is darker and grander, and became
the first (and, quite possibly, only) love song to an inflatable doll ever
broadcast on the John Peel show.

March 1973: Roxy Music – For Your Pleasure (LP)

Personnel:
Bryan Ferry: vocals, keyboards
Andy Mackay: sax
Phil Manzanera: guitar
Rick Porter: bass
Brian Eno: keyboards, electronics
Paul Thompson: drums
Produced by Chris Thomas, John Anthony, Roxy Music
Recorded AIR Studios, February 1973
Release date 23 March 1973
Highest chart positions: UK: 4, US:193
Tracks: 'Do The Strand', 'Beauty Queen', 'Strictly Confidential', 'Editions Of You',
'In Every Dream Home A Heartache', 'The Bogus Man', 'Grey Lagoons', 'For Your
Pleasure'

Back in November, Ferry told *New Musical Express* writer Nick Kent:

The next album is going to be the cheapest ever made. We're looking
for a really rough sound like on the original tracks we made for *Top*

Gear. One of the great things about speedy, cheap recording, is that you keep hearing odd little bits – mistakes and such which surface with each listening, and some of them are quite beautiful. Careful recording tends to sterilise sound to a great extent. Half the joy of those early Presley tracks was to be found in the primitive way they were recorded. We are actually using the Velvet's *White Light/White Heat* album as a fair example of what we eventually want. I'm not saying that we are going to sound like the Velvets in any way, it's just that we will probably use the same conditions they used to record that album. We hope to make it in a single afternoon.

In the event, wiser (and less parsimonious) heads prevailed: it took them two weeks. And from the moment needle hit vinyl, Roxy Music's second album swept away all the less-than-promising portents of a few months previous.

In Los Angeles at the end of 1972, Ferry fell into conversation with John Cale, who offered to produce the band's next LP. There were, Ferry admitted to *I. Mac*, 'a lot of practical difficulties at the moment. He wants to do it in L.A., you see. It'd be really nice working with him at some point'. Instead, they opted to co-produce with Chris Thomas, but still, there were some uncertainties.

Back in January – with the recording sessions still 'a couple of weeks' away – *New Musical Express*' Charles Shaar Murray repeated a rumour he'd heard: that the band was intending to re-record a bunch of songs from the first LP and release it as *Roxy Music's Greatest Hits*. Ferry simply remarked, 'I wouldn't deny it at this stage', and maybe that was his acknowledgement that there wasn't yet very much in the way of new songs. Once they were together in the studio, however, things happened fast. Songs happened fast.

Many regard *For Your Pleasure* as Roxy Music's finest hour, and some people were saying that, right from the start: '...a staggeringly fine piece of work', insisted Charles Shaar Murray's *New Musical Express* review, 'easily outstripping the first album. *For Your Pleasure* it's called, and damn if it ain't just that. Basically, it's a broadening of scope, and an extension of what has gone before. It's not simply a new set of songs in the same style, and it's not what musicians like to call 'a change of direction'. It's a new Roxy Music record, with all that implies'. Particularly when one focuses on its classics, which, incidentally, had already assumed that status before the album was even finished playing.

Side one both opens and closes with career-best drama. Perhaps that is why 'Do The Strand' and the blow-up-dolly delirium of 'In Every Dream Home A Heartache' were selected for showcasing on *The Old Grey Whistle Test* just days after the album's release (3 April). Both are included on the *The Thrill of it All* DVD.

Elsewhere, 'The Bogus Man' is serial-stalker spooky, while 'Editions Of You' simply rockets past – another of Ferry's beloved word salads, in which every lyric sparkles, particularly once he launches into the rapid-fire rap that concludes the cut. The band performed this song at the Golden Rose Festival in Montreux; footage is also available on *The Thrill of it All*.

If remaining cuts 'Beauty Queen', 'Strictly Confidential' and 'Grey Lagoons' have proven somewhat less memorable over the years, then they only fulfil the same role here as 'Chance Meeting' and 'Would You Believe?' occupied on the first album. And besides, we have still to address the album's title track – the conclusion to a second side that Charles Shaar Murray (again) described as 'a gruelling and disquieting experience along the lines of [David Bowie's] *The Man Who Sold The World*'. 'For Your Pleasure' was completely re-envisioned from the draggy Peel version of the previous November. Clad now in its funereal-dirge finest, it packs a portentous solemnity that utterly belies the pun that may or may not have been deliberately planted in the fade: the sound of Ferry bidding 'ta-ra', but to whom? We didn't have long to wait to find out. In mid-March – little more than two months after their last tour ended – Roxy were back on the road, albeit for a considerably shorter duration.

15 March 1973 University of Nottingham, Nottingham
16 March 1973 Hardrock, Manchester
17 March 1973 Sports Centre, Bracknell
18 March 1973 Town Hall, Birmingham
19 March 1973 De Montfort Hall, Leicester
24 March 1973 Guildhall, Plymouth
25 March 1973 Festival Hall, Torbay
27 March 1973 Trentham Gardens, Stoke
28 March 1973 City Hall, Sheffield
29 March 1973 City Hall, Newcastle
31 March-01 April 1973 Rainbow Theatre, London
04 April 1973 Guildhall, Preston
05 April 1973 Empire, Liverpool
06 April 1973 Green's Playhouse, Glasgow

07 April 1973 Odeon, Edinburgh
08 April 1973 Grand Theatre, Leeds
11 April 1973 Dome, Brighton
12 April 1973 Gaumont, Southampton
13 April 1973 Winter Gardens, Bournemouth
14 April 1973 Colston Hall, Bristol
15 April 1973 Capitol, Cardiff
23 April 1973 (unknown venue), Modena, Italy
24 April 1973 (unknown venue), Genova, Italy
29 April 1973 Golden Rose Festival, Montreux, Switzerland
03 May 1973 Rheinhalle, Dusseldorf, Germany
04 May 1973 Musikhalle, Hamburg, Germany
05 May 1973 Messehalle, Nurnberg, Germany
07 May 1973 (unknown venue), Munich, Germany
08 May 1973 Jarhunderthalle, Frankfurt, Germany
23 May 1973 Hallen, Kortrijk, Belgium
25 May 1973 De Doelen, Rotterdam, Holland
26 May 1973 Concertgebouw, Amsterdam, Holland

For Your Pleasure cover star Amanda Lear introduced the band onto
the stage across both nights at the Finsbury Park Rainbow, and Andrew
Tyler's review in *Disc* did its best to translate the ensuing spectacle to
printers ink: 'The stage itself – normally barren and vacant – was subtly
rearranged by use of a bank of spotlights that framed the band in the
centre spot. There were four dancing girls with dancing breasts'. Lear,
apparently, 'shook her things ... Bryan Ferry, the man with the upside-
down vocal cords, is fast becoming the star of the Roxy lineup and now
makes a separate flying entrance, and while onstage, collects much of the
attention. But there are plenty of visual distractions, not the least being
the bizarre couture and dancing feet'.

Melody Maker's Chris Charlesworth was also impressed: 'Gee, you
guys from Roxy sure do have style. Mmmmmmmm, yummy yummy. What I
couldn't do to that Bryan Ferry if he dropped around my place sometime.
He's so... er... and the way he... er... well, you know what I mean... so
fabulous. I saw them last night at The Rainbow, dear, and I'm speechless.
Talk about pleasure... wow, never mind about blowing that sexy little
bitch's mind, you blew mine too. Golly gee... let me tell you all about it...'.

In Germany, they made their debut on national television's *Musikladen*
– the first of four appearances over the next year or so, all of which have

seen the light of day via sundry releases through Radio Bremen. This one, however, is especially valuable for a rare glimpse of Ferry playing the white guitar that was strung around his white-suited neck through the first half of 'Dreamhome'.

There too, they met the German band Can, prompting guitarist Michael Karoli to tell the *New Musical Express*, 'They said they liked Can. All I know is that they liked my girlfriend a lot. And my sister too'.

In Paris, they took tea with Salvador Dali (Amanda Lear made the introductions).

The bootleggers were out in force as well. While sound quality remains a challenge, circulating tapes of Roxy's 17 March performances at the Bracknell Sports Centre and 7 May in Munich both indicate how powerful Roxy were at this point. Critics might complain that – Eno notwithstanding – they seldom deviated from the familiar studio takes, and it was often chance that pushed them further, as Richard Williams noted when he reviewed the Paris show for *Melody Maker*:

> There's no longer much to say about their act. It's exactly the same as we saw in Britain, and that's their policy. Nothing in the profile of the set is left to chance, only the audiences change. Either they like it, or they don't. It's the detail that keeps them interesting, fourth or fifth time around. Eno's treatment of the guitar and alto sax sound is always novel, often by accident. During 'Editions Of You', when his synthesizer conks out during the solos, he merely smiles.

But why should they have changed things around? What is the point of improving upon perfection?

And then it was all over. On 2 July, Roxy played the New York Festival in York. Days later, Eno quit. Ta-ra.

The split was announced in time for the 23 July inkies, and it seemed very magnanimous at first. 'I was cramping Eno's style', Ferry admitted. 'Two non-musicians in a band is one too many. I think he'll do very well by himself'. To which Eno replied, 'It was becoming a rather secure situation. It's characteristic of me – I even do it with girls – that when I reach a point of security, I quickly move out. But it's stimulating... I've had more ideas in the past three days than I've had for a year'.

The split did not especially surprise the band. As Phil Manzanera reflected, 'It was a very interesting combination of people that got together. We all had our own agendas, and when any one of those agendas got out of sync with the other peoples', like Eno's did with Bryan, then they sort of jumped ship'. At the time, the guitarist outlined a few flashpoints for the *New Musical Express*' Nick Kent: 'I remember the first actual blow-up occurring when Bryan held back on telling us that he'd designed the album sleeve of *For Your Pleasure*: which resulted in a huge argument on our coach'.

There were ego issues, as Eno acknowledged: 'Putting it as euphemistically as possible, Bryan felt the focus was divided by me being on stage, and that wasn't what he wanted. I'm beginning to think that strong personalities can only work together inside a casual relationship'.

Manzanera continued: 'It came to a head in America, which is only natural, particularly if you're not going down so well. We just felt it was an amazing drag. I mean, I could understand why Bryan got so upset really, because he was working amazingly hard on one side of the stage, and there was Eno on the other, grabbing all the attention because he looked so incredibly weird. We ended up trying to work out any number of solutions, but there was really no way out at all'.

Indeed, Eno's departure was only the first of what could've been a wholesale dissolution of the group, as Mackay and Manzanera also considered leaving. The guitarist continues:

> I was very good friends with Brian, and it did affect me a lot when he left. I almost left; I came very, very close, but in the end, at that point, I still wanted to be in a pop band that was being successful. It would have been perverse to quit, and that's when I realised there was an avenue to do both: to be in Roxy Music and to work with Eno.

As for Eno's first-publicised new project... there were so many of them. He talked of gathering anything up to six guitarists (Robert Fripp, Manzanera, Ritchie Blackmore, Tim Renwick and Mike Oldfield were among those he mentioned), whose guitars he would 'filter... through my approach. The whole thing would have a character of its own because I'd be the constant channel, but there'd also be variety'.

There was a various artists collection album that he'd already titled *Hysterical Hybrids And Musical Mutants*, for which he intended recruiting The Portsmouth Sinfonia, The Pan Am International Steel Band and sundry other left-field oddities. He talked of a proposed single with Phil Manzanera, and another with Andy Mackay: 'Never A Light Without A Shadow'. Manzanera was involved there, too, while the B-side would be another Mackay collaboration, this time with King Crimson's Boz Burrell, Mel Collins, Ian Wallace and sometime-Roxy-support-act Lloyd Watson. (Unfortunately, Eno admitted, 'I really can't remember what we decided to call (it)'.) 'We want to do lots (of singles), all in different styles. It's a Roxy spin-off really: the ideas we all had but couldn't do in the band', he told *Melody Maker*.

And there was Luana And The Lizard Ladies – doomed to non-appearance, however, because 'The girls haven't totally lizardised themselves yet. *I* could be Luana under the right circumstances'. Although, he also claimed to have been misquoted in the first place. The real name of the group, he told *New Musical Express*, was Loana and the Little Girls: 'Actually, that mistake has fired me to greater depths of inspiration, and every time I'm asked about the band, I call them something different, like... Lex Ligger and the Lozenges. My main idea is to drag together a bunch of bizarre people, who will probably all hate each other, give them some strange instrument to play, and get people to pay to watch them make fools of themselves'. This, too, was a nonstarter. When Eno did finally launch his post-Roxy career, it would be with the most uncompromising first shot imaginable. Or so he probably thought. In fact, Ferry had a left-field distraction of his own up his sleeve.

September 1973: Bryan Ferry – 'A Hard Rain's A-Gonna Fall' b/w '2HB' (Single) / October 1973: Bryan Ferry – These Foolish Things (LP)

Personnel:
Bryan Ferry: vocals, keyboards
John Porter: bass
Eddie Jobson: synth, violin
David Skinner: piano
Paul Thompson: drums)
Roger Ball, Malcolm Duncan, Henry Lowther: horns
Tracks: 'A Hard Rain's A-Gonna Fall', 'River Of Salt', Don't Ever Change', 'Piece Of My Heart', 'Baby I Don't Care', 'It's My Party', 'Don't Worry Baby', 'Sympathy For The Devil', 'The Tracks Of My Tears', 'You Won't See Me', 'I Love How You Love Me', 'Loving You Is Sweeter Than Ever', 'These Foolish Things'
Produced by Bryan Ferry, John Punter, John Porter
Recorded June 1973
LP Release date 5 October 1973
LP Highest chart positions UK: 5, US: did not chart

Single release date October 1973
Highest chart positions UK: 10, US: did not chart

Had Mackay and Manzanera jumped ship with Eno, this could very well have become the first album by the new-look Roxy Music. Thompson and Porter, after all, were familiar faces, while former Curved Air violinist Eddie Jobson and pianist Skinner (like Porter, ex-Uncle Dog) soon would be.

In the event, Roxy would emerge relatively unscathed from the turmoil. But alternative realities have their own appeal, regardless.

Ferry's debut solo single prefaced the main attraction: a brooding five-minute-plus assault on the decade-old Dylan classic that simultaneously extracted every last drop of Dylan-ness from both lyric and performance. A schoolfriend's penfriend best summed it up: 'I hate seeing him sing this on *Top of the Pops*. It was really frightening', or words to that effect.

Whatever the effect, Ferry achieved what nobody had (at that time) ever done to a Bob Dylan protest song. He transformed it from futuristic warning to apocalyptic newsflash, with little more than baleful keyboards and a voice that oozed dark obsession – which *was* the point, as Ferry confessed to *I. Mac*: 'I can't be bothered with all that Cuba Crisis stuff. I like the images'. Meanwhile, the record's ultimate top-five finish, marked the best performance yet for a Roxy-related 45.

These Foolish Things followed: the culmination of several weeks of quite unexpected rivalry between Ferry and David Bowie. Famously, Bowie too spent summer at work on a new album, and like Ferry, he chose to devote it wholly to cover versions – Bowie focussing on a narrow window in the mid-1960s; Ferry a more catholic (not to mention idiosyncratic) sweeping of songs dating back to 1935 (the title track), and forward to the end of the 1960s ('Sympathy For The Devil').

Bowie looked to The Who, The Yardbirds, Them, The Mojos and Pink Floyd for inspiration; Ferry favoured Goffin/King, Motown, The Beatles and The Beach Boys. And whereas Bowie played everything relatively straight, Ferry effectively rewired the history of modern pop around his own vocal and musical peculiarities. There was no correlation in the slightest between the two records, just two men having a similar idea at a similar time. But legal threats were proffered, regardless, with each party apparently assuming that the other was out to steal their thunder, and it was surely only the sheer stupidity of the entire feud that ultimately saw it sink from view. At least, one *hopes* that's what it was. (In fact, the only people who really had a bone to pick, were The Sweet. They'd been talking about making a covers record for over a year.)

Ferry was unrepentant, as he told the *New Musical Express* five years later: 'When I started doing other people's material, it was a bit misunderstood. People thought, 'Oh no, he wants to make commercial records'. For a start, there's nothing wrong with records that are commercially successful; some of the greatest records have terrible failures, and others have been smash hits. But the reason was simply that there are certain kinds of songs I can't write, that I wanted to perform'.

The absence of any fresh Ferry compositions did rankle some supporters, but it was also a cause for celebration. He was not, after all, the first frontman to launch a solo career parallel to a celebrated band: Rod Stewart, for one, was doing the same thing. But he was (and would – through the life of Roxy Music – remain) the only one who wasn't then torn over which strand of his career deserved the best songs.

The best performances, on the other hand: that was another matter entirely. *Creem*'s Ron Ross had one of the best takes on the album:

> Although some may complain that Ferry's renditions are too satirical to be taken seriously as alternative interpretations, Bryan's approach to oldies shows that he has great respect for their power to communicate certain timeless attitudes. By clever arrangements and vocal phrasing, he makes us more aware of what the songs are really saying, and at the same time, we learn to have fun with tunes we too often relate exclusively to the gymnasium dances and summer romances of yesteryear. And to prove that he can produce, arrange, and yes, sing with the best of them, Bryan has included a straightforwardly magnificent cover of The Beach Boys' 'Don't Worry Baby'.

The reference to satire is interesting, if only because it's difficult to decide whether that even crossed Ferry's mind as he was recording. Even within his own most sensitive lyrics, there is always the sense that he is having way too much fun with the sentimental imagery: the turtle doves of 'Pyjamarama'; the roses 'round the door in 'If There Is Something'. But is he truly mocking cliche? Or is that just what his voice does? If the former, then Ferry has never sung a sincere lyric in his life, because he brings the same quality to every single one of them… and that includes the put-downs. If the latter, then he's not guilty on all charges, and Phil Manzanera definitely comes down on that side of the debate: 'People used to think

Bryan was singing like that as a joke or something', he told *Trouser Press* in 1979. 'But it wasn't done on purpose: that was the real thing. I'm amazed that so many people think that Bryan was trying to do something affected'.

More than anything else, *These Foolish Things* is a courageous album. Not because a super groovy glam rock pop star was suddenly singing songs that your mother could like – and in 1973, that itself was a pretty damning stance – but because he was singing songs that most of his peers would've left in the shower because that was the only place where they could get away with them.

Nowhere was this more in evidence than when the album reached its conclusion. Ferry's take on the title track could – nay, *should* – have been a shipwreck. He was following, after all, in the footsteps of some of pre-rock pop's most storied vocalists: Bing Crosby and Frank Sinatra among them. But when writer Robert Cushman retold the song's recorded history for editor Tim de Lisle's 1994 book *The Lives Of The Great Songs*, he had no hesitation in proclaiming Ferry's version among the greatest of them all, and not simply because it's 'textually the fullest'. Ferry, writes Cushman, 'sings out of tempo, in traditional verse manner, but he's backed by a piercing trumpet and exaggeratedly docile piano: a Brecht and Weill combination. All the elements of the song are laid out – the elegance, the nonchalance, the driven misery – but dislocated and jumbled ... Ferry's sweet-sour version might be the one I play on my platonic ideal of a radio programme'.

Interestingly, of the 36 songs included in *The Lives of the Great Songs*, Ferry had (or now has) recorded no less than four: 'These Foolish Things' is joined by 'Take Me To The River', 'I Put A Spell On You' and 'The Tracks Of My Tears', and one can readily imagine him taking a stab at several others (How 'I'll Be Your Baby Tonight' never made *Dylanesque* is an utter mystery). Clearly, the man has impeccable taste.

More than that, though, he knew his own worth: 'I've given up trying to please all of the people all of the time', he told the *New Musical Express* as the album hit the shops. 'Some will like it for one reason, some for another. And some will presumably dislike it for the wrong reasons, though I hope the general point of it will be understood. Its amusement value'. Which Greg Shaw – writing for *Phonograph Record* – immediately translated into language that anyone could understand:

> For weeks, I'd been hearing how bad this album was from people whose judgment is usually reliable. How pleasant then to discover an album so

disarmingly ludicrous, that it'll probably end up one of my favorite dumb records of all time, right alongside *The Cowsills in Concert* and *Best of The Iron Butterfly*. If nothing else, it's better than Dylan'.

November 1973: Roxy Music – 'Street Life' b/w'Hula Kula' (Single)/ November 1973: Roxy Music – Stranded (LP)

Personnel:
Bryan Ferry: vocals, keyboards
Andy Mackay: sax
Phil Manzanera: guitar
John Gustafson: bass
Chris Thomas: bass
Eddie Jobson: keyboards, synthesizer
Paul Thompson: drums
Chris Laurence: double bass
London Welsh Male Choir
Produced by Chris Thomas
Recorded AIR, London, September 1973
LP Release date 1 November 1973
Highest chart positions (album): UK: 1, US: 186
Highest chart positions (single): UK: 9, US: did not chart
Tracks: 'Street Life', 'Just Like You', 'Amazona', 'Psalm', 'Serenade', 'A Song For Europe', 'Mother Of Pearl', 'Sunset'

Eno, it is said, later described *Stranded* as Roxy Music's best album, although it's doubtful that he'll find too many fans who agree with him: not even among those who ensured it became the band's first UK chart-topper. Over at the *New Musical Express*, I. Mac too was delighted with it: '*Stranded* is a classic – the album Roxy have been aiming at for two years, and the long-awaited firm ground for the group's fans to stand on, even if some of the subtleties of the earlier approach have had to go, in order to get there'.

But again, was it really that good? Or were we just thrilled that the band had survived the sundering and still sounded much the same? 'Eno's gone', mused I. Mac, 'taking most of the overt craziness with him, and allowing Ferry to develop his own mood, free from the worry of having to accommodate a totally different creative temperament (viz., the synthesizer break on 'Editions Of You')'. At last, he continued, Ferry could 'give full reign to his *very* different obsessions. The Great Break-Up, in other words, has turned out to be A Good Thing...'.

Across the ocean, *Circus* was equally admiring: 'When Brian Eno left Roxy Music', wrote Michael Gross, 'something was lost that can never be retrieved by the band. His bizarre inspiration cannot be matched by any other musician (or, as he preferred, non-musician). But the addition of Eddie Jobson gave Roxy something they didn't have before: a new sound to play with. It doesn't make up for Eno's loss, but the fact is that Eno was not essential to Roxy',

Neither, in business terms, was Jobson, or so he seemed to think: 'I (joined) on a sort-of session basis', he told New Musical Express' Chris Salewicz. 'I'm a permanent member, but at the same time, I'm completely free. I'm not signed to anybody. I'm paid on a session basis. I get a wage and fees for doing concerts, and a fee for doing albums rather than collecting royalties. It means that they can fire me whenever they want. And it also means that I can walk out whenever I want'. Hopefully, that wouldn't happen for a while.

The single 'Street Life' boded extraordinarily well, fading in on sounds that could almost be said to echo the party atmosphere of 'Re-make/Re-model', before erupting into one of Ferry's now-characteristic mach-2 kaleidoscopes of word and imagery. True, it didn't quite match the white jacket and black dickie bow which accompanied him onto the 22 November edition of *Top of the Pops*, but Eddie Jobson's see-through violin was as great a distraction as anything Eno ever wore.

And maybe that was *Stranded*'s problem. It was *too* characteristic. Or, at least, it was devoid of the surprises with which its predecessors had been littered. Jobson acquits himself well; his grandiose piano an especial joy. And Ferry's songwriting, if taken in the word's literal meaning, is strong. The songs that did raise *Stranded* to fresh heights, truly soared. So what if 'Psalm' needs four minutes of slow-burn buildup before all hell is let loose by band and singer alike. Ferry is almost literally swinging his voice around his head, Mackay appears to be honking several tunes simultaneously, and one can only imagine what would've happened had it only been granted a harder, sharper, more dramatic production.

'Mother Of Pearl' – one of the two songwriting credits that Ferry shared on the album (There's a first time for everything) – can best be described today as the ultimate punk/prog hybrid, as visualised by a modern-jazz barbershop quartet. Co-writer Phil Manzanera is certainly responsible for the frantic first half; Ferry steps in with what emerges as a gloriouslylouche lyric ('I've been up all night again') and a looping coda that felt even more distinguished after Simple Minds borrowed its form for their own 'Chelsea Girl'.

And then there's 'A Song For Europe': a Ferry/Mackay co-write that makes you wish they'd collaborated far more frequently. Less a song, more a forgotten epic of *noir* cinema, the only question is, who is the singer mourning? A lost girlfriend? Or a vanished civilisation? The clue might fall when Ferry goes all Rosetta Stone on us and sings two final verses: first in Latin, and then in French. And suddenly, one wishes Roxy had released this as their Christmas single. The vision of 'A Song For Europe' battling for honours with Steeleye Span's own Latin sing-along 'Gaudete', could've rewired *Top of the Pops* for years to come.

As it is, schoolboy French classes became a lot more interesting that autumn and winter of 1973, as author Michael Collins (*The Likes of Us* (2004)) reminds us: 'When Bryan Ferry sang 'tous ce moments/Perdus dans l'enchantement', French lessons temporarily appealed. It was worth showing up to get a translation'.

That was the good news. Unfortunately, there were also some bad tidings. The band's second LP of the year, *Stranded* was recorded almost as quickly as its predecessor. But this time, it shows. The need to bed in two new boys (Jobson was joined by ex-Quatermass bassist John Gustafson, who replaced John Porter for the last tour) as quickly as possible while adhering to Island's demand for a new album for Christmas, ensured that *Stranded* was always going to be a rush job.

Had the core quartet been allowed more time and, perhaps, familiarity with the lineup change, even the ultra-tedious 'Just Like You' might have been arranged into something approaching a riot. And it's not alone – if the remainder of *Stranded* truly deserves comparison with any past Roxy offering, 'Sunset', 'Amazona' and 'Serenade' (which tries so hard to rock, but ultimately barely rolls across the carpet) have the most in common with the versions of 'Beauty Queen', 'For Your Pleasure' and 'The Bogus Man' that the band took for a live test drive in late 1972.

They're not quite demos, but they're certainly not the finished article, and if *Stranded* regularly made it into the uppermost reaches of the end-of-the-year polls, that might be more down to the weakness of the competition (particularly among the bands that truly were Roxy's competition at the time) than to the strength of the album itself. For all the acclaim that nostalgia drips down upon it, 1973 was *not* a vintage year for long-playing records.

With that in mind, it is sometimes worth remembering just how far ahead of the pack Roxy Music were at this time. Noting how *These Foolish Things* beat Bowie – the generally accepted market leader of the era – to the *covers-album* concept by a clear three months, it's also worth noting that the often-apocalyptic *Stranded* had a similar head start over Bowie's doom-laden *Diamond Dogs*. Indeed, Roxy Music were to both outlast and outsell Bowie, at least in terms of maintaining a glam rock sheen. While Bowie moved from the delicious, spiraling tease of *Aladdin Sane* to the hard rock of *Diamond Dogs* and on to the plastic soul of *Young Americans*, Roxy, Ferry and – in his early solo career – Eno, were all to continue along the lines laid down by their first tentative attempts to cross teenage revolution with Fritz Lang's *Metropolis*.

Even after the glam genre itself had run its course, and Ferry was flirting with a succession of new styles and images (including the gaucho look, which single-handedly inspired the *New Musical Express*' long-running 'Lone Groover' cartoon strip), Roxy Music continued to signpost the direction things might have gone had only the rest of the pack not drifted off in search of other, safer, harbours.

They couldn't help it. Even today, Bryan Ferry wears a Hollywood glamour sheen; a veneer the impression of being out on the edge. He redefined decadence at a time when most people were still trying to find out what it used to mean. It's just that sometimes he took it a little too far. *Melody Maker*'s Michael Watts put it well:

> Roxy Music evoke on this album an impression of lush melancholy, full of elusive bittersweet fragrances. I can see why some critics find it hard to like them while appreciating what they do. Their music isn't warm or embracing. Here it's suffused with an exotic Poe-like quality that distances the creators from their listener, while Ferry's strange voice lends it the chill bloom of the corpse.

Ken Barnes, at America's *Phonograph Record*, declared:

> Though I liked the first two Roxy Music albums reasonably well, *Stranded* is the first one that's immediately impressed me … Aside from its initial impressive qualities, (it) is even better on further listenings. On each play, more oddball lyric lines or weirdly-effective atonalities, pop out, and it's all definitely a treat; effete but quite neat and with a beat.

Only Nick Kent – of all the UK music press' most sainted seers – seemed to sense that something was amiss, and even *he* waited a year until his review of the band's *fourth* album before sticking his head above the parapet. He still called *Stranded* 'truly wonderful', but he also acknowledged that it was 'something of a flawed *meisterwerk*'.

November 1973: Roxy Music – Live at The Rainbow (US TV)

Personnel:
Bryan Ferry: vocals, keyboards
Andy Mackay: sax
Phil Manzanera: guitar
Sal Maida: bass
Eddie Jobson: keyboards, synthesizer
Paul Thompson: drums
Tracks: 'Editions Of You', 'A Song For Europe', 'Do The Strand'

Although no footage from the Rainbow show has been officially released, it was at least partially filmed for broadcast on US television. All three songs subsequently appeared on the *Better Than Food* bootleg; 'Editions Of You' and 'Do The Strand' also featured on another fondly-remembered boot: *Champagne and Novocaine*.

The band lineup had undergone another shift. John Gustafson was unavailable for the tour, and with less than a month to go, the band was still searching for a replacement. Enter New Yorker Sal Maida. Maida recalls: 'I originally went to London with the intention of getting into an English band because I'd always been a big Anglophile, so I started going to auditions. I auditioned for Family, jammed with Davy O'List, I auditioned for this band called Hard Stuff, and this other band called Spring, things like that, answering ads in *Melody Maker*, talking with musicians at the Speakeasy, stuff like that'.

He almost tried out for Sparks, too, shortly after Ron and Russell Mael relocated to London. Maida had already seen the group in New York in 1971; now they were putting together a new lineup in London, 'and they had an ad in *Melody Maker*: I believe it said 'English musicians only', but I thought I'd call anyway ... 'Mmm, we're here looking for English guys and we don't want to go through the work permit thing, the visa thing'.

However, Maida already had his eyes set on another band entirely:

I'd seen Roxy do 'In Every Dream Home A Heartache' on the Whistle Test, and I was totally mind-blown. 'This is the greatest band ever! Great music, they look great…', and I thought, 'This is the band for me. So I started investigating, and when For Your Pleasure came out, I saw on the cover, 'Guest artiste, John Porter – bass', so I (thought), 'Alright, these guys have existed for two years and already they've had three bass players', so maybe I have a shot at it. Anyway, I was working in the Scene and Heard record store, and Paul Thompson came in. Now, I'd done a session with Paul about a year or two before that, and we remembered each other … 'Wow, you're in that band, great band', and he (said) 'Well, we may be looking for somebody to go on the road and play bass.

Thompson had come into the shop looking for a copy of Family's *Old Songs New Songs* album. Maida thought fast:

We had it in stock, but me being devious and wanting to get an audition for this band, I told him we didn't have it, but I'd order it for him, hoping it'd get him back to the store. And it worked great because he came back to the store two days later, and Eddie Jobson was with him. So I said, 'Yeah, we've got the record', and he said, 'We're definitely looking for someone, so come down to AIR Studios to audition'. This was August, early September, and they'd be going out about a month later. I went down and they were mixing Stranded, so it was kinda chaotic because the label wanted the record done and they were still mixing. I went up again, and it was a very nerve-wracking experience because they were so under-the-gun with scheduling for the record, that they didn't have time to audition me. But the good part was I got to know them, we'd talk, they'd ask me stuff, we'd just hang out, and finally, the third time I went up to AIR, I went in with Paul, just bass and drums. And we started playing, and on the other side of the glass, there was the whole band and Chris Thomas the producer. Paul and I played for about 20 minutes, and when we were done, the band (said) 'Great, you've got the gig. Go see our manager tomorrow, sort out money and wardrobe and whatever'. It was pretty amazing.

14 October 1973 (unknown venue) Bath
19 October 1973 Leeds University, Leeds
21 October 1973 Town Hall, Birmingham
22 October 1973 City Hall, Sheffield

23 October 1973 St Georges Hall, Bradford
26 October 1973 Empire Theatre, Liverpool
27 October 1973 University Of Nottingham
28 October 1973 Free Trade Hall, Manchester
30 October 1973 de Montfort Hall, Leicester
02 November 1973 Green's Playhouse, Glasgow
03 November 1973 Empire Theatre, Edinburgh
04 November 1973 City Hall, Newcastle
05 November 1973 Colston Hall, Bristol (Cancelled)
06 November 1973 Winter Gardens, Bournemouth
08 November 1973 Brangwyn Hall, Swansea Wales
10-12 November 1973 Rainbow Theatre, London
14 November 1973 Olympen, Lund, Sweden
15 November 1973 Tivoli Concert Hall, Copenhagen, Denmark
16 November 1973 Concerthaus, Gothenburg, Sweden
20 November 1973 Audi Max, Hamburg, Germany
21 November 1973 Jahrhunderthalle, Frankfurt, Germany
22 November 1973 Rheinhalle, Dusseldorf, Germany
23 November 1973 (unknown venue) Berlin, Germany
24 November 1973 Circus Kroner, Munich, Germany
26 November 1973 (unknown venue) Genoa, Italy
29 November 1973 Brancaccio, Rome, Italy
01 December 1973 Vienna Concerthaus, Austria
04 December 1973 Nancy pars des Expositions, Nancy, France
06 December 1973 Cinema Marni, Brussels, Belgium
07 December 1973 Doelen, Rotterdam, Netherlands
08 December 1973 Concertgebouw, Amsterdam, Netherlands
10 December 1973 Palais des Sports, Paris, France
11 December 1973 Palais d'Hiver, Lyons, France
12 December 1973 (unknown venue) Poitiers, France
16 December 1973 Theatre Royal, Bath
18 December 1973 Colston Hall, Bristol (Rescheduled date)
20 February 1974 (unknown venue) Boston, Massachusetts
04-05 April 1974 Floral Hall, Southport

Maida accompanied the band on tours of Europe and the UK, and the Maels – who were *still* in the throes of putting a band together – came to one of the three Rainbow gigs. Of course, Maida said 'Hi' when they arrived backstage.

With the European tour complete, Maida returned to New York before being recalled to action six months later. At the end of May – a year and a half after their first US visit – Roxy Music kicked off what they described as their second American tour, but which in reality was little more than a fact-finding mission. It was, after all, just five shows long.

25 May 1974 Ford Auditorium, Detroit, MI
26 May 1974 Allen Theatre, Cleveland, OH
29 May 1974 The Roxy Theater, Northampton, PA
31 May 1974 Painter's Mill Theatre, Owings Mills, MD
02 June 1974 Academy of Music, New York NY

Things had improved a lot since the 1972 visit: now people wanted to see Roxy Music, and they enjoyed the show accordingly. Nevertheless, critics remained bemused. The *New York Times* review of the Academy of Music show, remarked simply, 'On Sunday, (Ferry) appeared in slick back black hair, black tie, white summer formal jacket and a red cummerbund, looking for all the world like Desi Arnaz playing Brighton'.

America's refusal to fully embrace Roxy Music is not hard to understand. In a land where – well ahead of the modern preoccupation with generic pigeonholing – music could be sold only if there was an audience for the pluggers to target it towards, Roxy Music teased too many tastes and satisfied none. They were art rock, they were glam rock, and with Bryan Ferry now sporting tuxedos and singing 'Smoke Gets In Your Eyes', they were even pre-rock – no wonder many people opted to simply close their eyes to the whole thing and write them off as just another obscure European thing.

Chapter Five: Dignified by the Loop

November 1973: Fripp & Eno – (No Pussyfooting) (Album)

Personnel:

Robert Fripp, Brian Eno

Produced by Brian Eno, Robert Fripp

Recorded Eno's home studio; Maida Vale, London; Command Studios, London, 8 September 1972, 4–5 August 1973

Release date November 1973

Highest chart positions: did not chart

Tracks: 'The Heavenly Music Corporation', 'Swastika Girls'

2008 bonus tracks: 'The Heavenly Music Corporation' (half speed), 'Swastika Girls' (Half speed), 'The Heavenly Music Corporation' (Reversed), 'Swastika Girls' (Reversed)

Fripp and Eno met for the first time during the debut album sessions for Robert Wyatt and Bill MacCormick's new band Matching Mole. Eno – who knew Wyatt from a Peter Schmidt art exhibition they both attended during summer 1972 – was recruited to add VCS3 to one track – 'Gloria Gloom' – where it sets up an eerie wash behind fellow guest actress Julie Christie's monotone vocal. 'I liked his synth work', says MacCormick. 'Dave (Pianist Dave McRae) was a bit put out when he arrived with his VCS3, but (Brian) wasn't there to play keyboard parts, but add the loops etc. on 'Gloria Gloom', so it wasn't really an issue'.

The rest of Eno's time was spent at the mixing desk, watching producer Fripp at work, and shortly after the sessions wrapped in late August, Fripp was visiting Eno at his Leith Mansions home, laying down the first of the electronic meanderings that would ultimately be resolved as *(No Pussyfooting)*: an album – Eno later learned – that David Bowie claimed he could hum.

(No Pussyfooting) was both utterly opposed to anything that fans of Roxy Music (or even King Crimson) might've expected to fork out hard cash for, and an exquisite indication of where Roxy Music at least could themselves have journeyed, at least for a short while: a point proven when Ferry presented the not-entirely-dissimilar 'Sultanesque' for a 1975 B-side. Eno explained to Mojo in 1995:

> It was the two of us making one sound. (Fripp) did all the clever stuff
> for sure, but the sound that he was hearing was routed through my

machinery, I was changing it and he was responding to what I was doing. This was really a new idea, the notion that two people could make one sound in that way. That kind of got me into the idea of the studio not as a place for reproducing music but as a place for changing it or recreating it from scratch.

As a precursor to the 'ambient' genre that Eno would both birth and pioneer a couple of years later, the importance of *(No Pussyfooting)* is inestimable. No matter that more than one critic allied it to the sound of two robots arguing over whose turn it is to take out the trash – *(No Pussyfooting)* would prove to be a peerless tutor to that still-youthful generation of kids that would come of age in the post-punk era of cheap synths and ice blasts, and would open a lot of other doors as well, including the one that led to another of Eno's collaborations: with David Bowie in 1976/1977. In the event, it would be the ensuing *Low* that would take the credit for electrifying the punk generation's fascination with machines. But without *(No Pussyfooting)*, even the Bowie albums might not have happened.

Late-1973 also saw the release of another Eno project, as he both played on and produced the debut album by The Portsmouth Sinfonia: *...Plays The Popular Classics*.

The Sinfonia's reputation and popularity had been increasing wildly in the year since ICES. By 1973, the Sinfonia was playing the Purcell Rooms at the Royal Festival Hall, but even for the initiated, *Plays The Popular Classics* can be a challenge to sit through. There are, after all, only so many wrong notes that one can listen to before Bryars' intended 'clouds of sound' instead become a ragged mass of irritability and headache. But the Sinfonia's take on 'Jupiter' from Gustav Holst's *The Planets* suite is tremendous under any regime, as the hymn 'I Vow To Thee My Country' is transformed into something best described as the sound of a hippo very slowly rising and stretching itself before settling down to do it again.

Occasionally the music does veer into joke territory – most notably when tackling pieces that are so well-known that it is impossible to actually damage them (Beethoven's 5th and the accompanying single – the long-suffering 'William Tell Overture' are examples). But the Sugar Plum Fairy, dances not only with lead boots but a diving helmet too, and if *this* is what morning sounds like, it's a wonder that we aren't all nocturnal.

January 1974: Brian Eno – Here Come The Warm Jets (Album)

Personnel:

Brian Eno: vocals, synth, keyboards, treatments, guitars etc.

Chris Spedding: guitar

Phil Manzanera: guitar

Bill MacCormick: bass

Robert Fripp: guitar

Paul Rudolph: guitar, bass

John Wetton: bass

Andy Mackay: sax, keyboards

Paul Thompson: drums

Lloyd Watson: slide guitar

+ others

Produced by Eno

Recorded Majestic Studios, London, September 1973

Release date January 1974

Highest chart positions: UK: 26, US: did not chart

Tracks: 'Needle In The Camel's Eye', 'The Paw Paw Negro Blowtorch', 'Baby's On Fire', 'Cindy Tells Me', 'Driving Me Backwards', 'On Some Faraway Beach', 'Blank Frank', 'Dead Finks Don't Talk', 'Some Of Them Are Old', 'Here Come The Warm Jets'

With *(No Pussyfooting)* in the stores and attracting curious glances wherever it was sighted (it had a terrific sleeve, after all), Eno then body-swerved back to something approaching conventional song, and cut an album that could actually have *been* Roxy Music if it had been *Ferry* who felt he had to go. Eno even used the same band in places – Mackay, Manzanera and Thompson all performed on the record, and while Manzanera doesn't remember if it bothered Ferry to see his bandmates' loyalties so clearly split, he admits, 'I suppose it must have done. Either I was oblivious to it, or he was busy enough not to notice'.

At the same time, however, the guitarist admits it was a hectic time, as he found himself working 'six hours a day in Clapham with Eno, then going up to Oxford Circus to work six hours a day on *Stranded*. I didn't shout about it, of course, but that was a strange period'.

Among the other guests, Chris Spedding was one of the country's fastest-rising young guitar heroes, with stints alongside John Cale and

Bryan Ferry in his future. Paul Rudolph was a former Pink Fairy, and Lloyd Watson had of course, supported Roxy Music on tour.

There was also a role for Quiet Sun/Matching Mole's Bill MacCormick, who remembers being 'very surprised to be asked to the *Warm Jets* session. Hadn't really been playing much and was a bit rusty, but the parts were not exactly challenging. All a great laugh, though. The only thing I can think of is that the Hammond organ part at the end of 'Blank Frank' is about five of us all playing a few randomly chosen notes simultaneously'.

Here Come the Warm Jets is an almost absurdly-accessible record, even allowing for the less-than-sanitary undertones of its title. Ray Fox-Cummings in *Disc* acknowledged 'Some people may well complain that the album is infuriatingly frivolous, which, in a way, some of it is. But I wouldn't squabble on that account, because it is genuinely funny where it sets out to be, and the music is perfectly valid throughout'.

Either 'Baby's On Fire' or 'Driving Me Backwards' could easily have been unveiled as singles, with Fox-Cummings pointing out regarding the former: '(It) has a lot to thank *The Rocky Horror Show* for – not only does the tune sound familiar, but the vocal is just like Riff Raff: a character in the show, who incidentally is the spitting image of Eno'.

'Cindy Tells Me' sounds like it ought to be a ballad, and the quick-fire imagery of Eno's often absurdist lyricism sets up pictures in the mind that no other songwriter could ever have conceived.

If the first side of the record left you breathless, side two could stop your heart. The five songs of the semi-suite – not quite themed, but not too distant from one another either – begin with the deathbed hopefulness of 'On Some Faraway Beach' – the suite winding its way to the pulsating title track through both visions and notions like the craziest paving.

'Blank Frank' – co-written with Fripp – is barked suggestion and imprecation; 'Dead Finks Don't Talk' is military precision overlaid with nursery nonsense that only slowly resolves itself into one of the most cruel love songs you have ever encountered, without it even admitting that it is one: 'To be a zombie all the time requires such dedication'. It also packs an ending that still defies expectations almost 50 years of repeated listenings later. All the better to shock you into the tender – even regretful – pastures of 'Some Of Them Are Old' – a song that more than one listener has suggested could've been written for Roxy Music, but which quickly packs the lachrymosity away to teeter instead on the sonic mysteries of pre-war Shanghai and the ghosts of imperial ballrooms:

or – in other words – precisely the kind of territory that Bryan Ferry marked for his own. At least, that's one interpretation. Every listener has their own; some of us have several. 'The album's feeling is more important than its concepts and subtleties', insisted Richard Cromelin in *Phonograph Record*:

It's mysterious; nonspecific; it keeps you off balance with an elusive focus that slips from your grasp like quicksilver. Songs like 'Cindy Tells Me', 'On Some Faraway Beach' and 'Some Of Them Are Old' are evocative, touching pieces, much more genuine and sincere than we'd expect from an artist who is generally portrayed as a flippant soul. Here the John Cale influence dominates – dreamy atmospheres, augmented vocals, simple supremely lovely melodies; involved spacious arrangements.

Whatever your opinion, *Here Come The Warm Jets* set Eno up as one of *the* stars-most-likely-to in 1974, and no sooner was the album complete than plans were being laid for him to tour. Nobody had any doubt that, with the right musicians behind him, Eno could easily establish himself alongside Roxy Music – another reason for Ferry to be grateful that his own bandmates were back on board the mothership now with their upcoming American tour to worry about.

So Eno looked elsewhere.

13 February 1974: Brian Eno and The Winkies – King's Hall, Derby

Personnel:
Brian Eno: vocals, keyboards
Guy Humphreys, Phil Rambow: guitar
Brian Turrington: bass
Mike Desmarais: drums
Tracks: 'Blank Frank', 'Needle In The Camel's Eye', 'Dead Finks Don't Talk', 'Dignified By The Loop', 'Love Slips Away', 'Here Come The Warm Jets', 'Fever', 'I'm A Boy', 'What Goes On', 'The Paw Paw Negro Blowtorch', 'Baby's On Fire', 'I'll Come Running', 'Seven Deadly Finns', 'I Go Ape'

Whereas the smart money would've been on Eno selecting a backing band from among the like-minded souls who appeared on the album, he clearly had other thoughts. An early attempt to convince R&B sledgehammer Dr Feelgood to tour with him was rebuffed. He turned instead to The

Winkies: the Feelgoods' fellow pub rockers who Eno encountered for the first time at the Brecknock, Camden Town, in November 1973. The band – which had only been playing live for a month – were initially divided over the offer, but guitarist Phil Rambow was adamant: 'I loved Eno, I thought he was great. Whatever he wanted to do would be fun, so we negotiated: we'd do our set and then come on and do his. We'd record together, he'd produce us, and it became a marriage made in heaven creatively. Plus, he really liked our playing'.

Rehearsals began immediately, and Eno had just one requirement. Rambow continues: 'He told us, 'You can play anything you want on any of my songs, just don't ever play the blues. Whenever you even come close to even trying to sound like a blues note, just don't do it'. So everything we did with him, there was this little jewel of instruction, and that's what makes him so great as a producer and someone to work with'.

The team also went into the studio to cut three numbers – Eno's 'Seven Deadly Finns', a distinctly loopy cover of 'The Lion Sleeps Tonight', and the proposed first Winkies single: a Rambow original called 'Last Chance'. The first would become Eno's first single, premiered with an appearance on the Dutch *Toppop* TV show at the beginning of January; the latter was canned when The Winkies' label Chrysalis rejected it out of hand. The release was abandoned, but further recordings were planned for once the tour was over. That opportunity would come a lot sooner than anybody expected.

Twenty shows were booked, and the live set offers a fascinating glimpse into the mind of Eno, the potential pop star. Opening with 'Blank Frank', it comprised a little more than half of *Here Come the Warm Jets* interspersed with a few favourite covers – the Velvets' 'What Goes On' (which Bryan Ferry would pointedly cover himself four years later), Peggy Lee's 'Fever', and a petulant proto-punk reimagining of The Who's 'I'm A Boy'. There were two new songs – 'Love Slips Away' and 'Dignified By The Loop' – and an encore of Neil Sedaka's 'I Go Ape'.

Eno hated every minute of the experience.

He sounds fabulous. Retune your ears around the horrendous murk that is the only circulating recording from the tour – at Derby's King's Hall on 13 February 1974 – and it's easy to foresee a vivid future for the package. As Rambow recalls, 'Rehearsals were fine, everybody was really looking forward to getting on the road, including Brian'. But then came the first night:

He hated being in the centre of the stage: in the spotlight with a synth and having to sing the same things we'd rehearsed. That great look he had with Roxy Music – the mad professor on the side with the feathers: that was gone. In its place was the naked man in the spotlight. You could see he didn't like it. It was just too limiting as a lifestyle, and required too much of a discipline that he didn't have.

Eno agreed. He told *Trouser Press* in 1977, 'Jumping around the stage is the most self-conscious activity for me. I knew it was the wrong decision from the first night of the tour'.

Worse was to come at either the second or third show. Eno was introducing the band; Rambow recalls: 'He went through us… Guy, Phil, Brian… and he comes to the last of us, and from the back of the crowd, this huge great voice comes booming out: 'And who the fuck are you?'. That was the beginning of the end'.

The tour ground on – Sheffield, Swansea, Bristol, Dunstable, and then disaster, as Eno was suddenly rushed into hospital with a collapsed right lung. 'It was the only project I've been involved in during the last few years that I would say was abortive', Eno continued in the *Trouser Press* interview:

But I decided that I didn't want to be a star: the kind of figure Bryan became. I knew that becoming that, would only inhibit what I really wanted to do, because my ideas are so diverse and frequently apparently unrelated, that I need a low-profile position from which to produce them. The momentum of my career had been toward becoming a sub-David Bowie. But what I like is sitting in little rooms and fiddling with things until they suddenly hit a chord.

March 5, 1974: Eno and The Winkies – Top Gear (BBC Radio) / March 1974: Brian Eno – Seven Deadly Finns' b/w 'Later On' (Single)

Personnel (Session + A-side):
Brian Eno: vocals, electronics
Philip Rambow: guitar
Brian Turrington: bass
Guy Humphreys: guitar
Mike Desmarais: drums (B-side: see No Pussyfooting (above))

Above: The glammest gang in town, circa 1972…

Below: … and circa 1975.

Left: Phil Manzanera's 2001 rarities collection looked back to the first *Quiet Sun* demos. (*BMG*)

Right: 'The answer to a maiden's prayer' - quite possibly the greatest debut album of all time. (*Island / Reprise*)

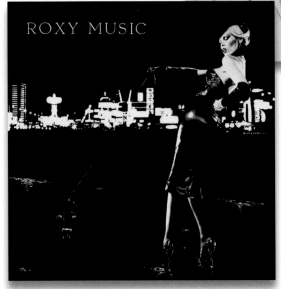

Left: *For Your Pleasure.* The 'difficult' second album proved not to be so hard, after all. (*Island / Warner Bros*)

Right: Ferry sings your mum and dad's favourites (and maybe some of grandma's, too). (*Island*)

Left: *Stranded*. Eno's out, Jobson's in, but Roxy march on regardless. (*Island / Atco*)

Right: *(No Pussyfooting)* - and David Bowie could apparently whistle the entire thing. (*Island / EG*)

Left: Rumour notwithstanding, Eno insists the album was named for a treatment he created called 'warm jet guitar'. (*Island*)

Right: *Another Time, Another Place*. Bryan Ferry, by the pool, with a tux. The ultimate Cluedo cover. (*Island*)

Left: From 'The Long and Winding Road' to 'Ride of the Valkyries' - Eddie Riff certainly travelled far. (*Island*)

Right: *Country Life*. Roxy's fourth album cover was banned in America. (*Island / Atco*)

Left: *Taking Tiger Mountain (By Strategy)*. '...a brilliant record. But it is brilliant under its own terms.' (*Island*)

Right: It took 46 years to appear on disc, but now we can all attend Bryan's first solo live show. (*BMG*)

BRYAN FERRY

Live at the
ROYAL ALBERT HALL
1974

Left: Mackay and Manzanera on *The Old Grey Whistle Test*, 1972.

Right: Was this Bryan's greatest jacket? *The Old Grey Whistle Test*, 1972.

Left: Eno knows what this button will do. But does anybody else?

Right: The King of Cool!

Left: German TV, 1974, performing 'All I Want Is You.' The absence of a bassist apparently made no difference.

Right: Eddie Jobson and Phil Manzanera on German TV in 1975.

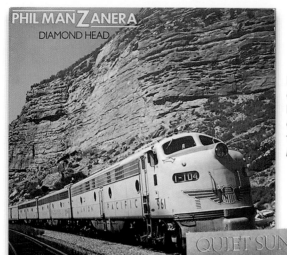

Left: Phil Manzanera: 'I went off to Basing Street Studios and booked it from twelve to twelve, and everyone said fine. From twelve to six I did *Diamond Head...*' (*Island / Atco*)

Right: '..., [and] from six to twelve I did *Quiet Sun*'. (*Island*)

Left: Get your 'Sombre Reptiles' here. The third Brian Eno album. (*Island*)

Right: *Siren*. Jerry Hall on the Anglesey coast. (*Island / Atco*)

EVENING STAR FRIPP & ENO

Left: Fripp and Eno's second album includes what one biographer called their most 'sustained tonal experiment yet.' (*Island*)

ROCK FOLLIES

Right: Andy Mackay wrote and produced the soundtrack to this 1976 ITV series. (*Island / Atlantic*)

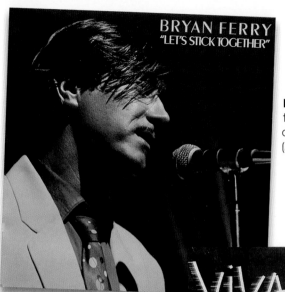

Left: Most people call it Ferry's third solo album. But it was actually his first B-sides collection. (*EG*)

Right: *Viva* could, and should, have been a double album. Instead, it became Roxy's (first) epitaph. (*Island*)

Left: 'If it wasn't for tumultuous waves of applause phasing in and out, *Live* could pass for a studio album' - *Sounds*. (*Island*)

Right: Eno meets Kraut Rock. (*Groenland*)

Harmonia & Eno '76
Tracks and Traces *reissue*

MUSIC FOR FILMS   BRIAN ENO

Left: The 1978 release of Eno's *Music for Films* gave official status to a 1976 promo. (*EG*)

Right: Maybe not the movie world's greatest idea - an all-covers Beatles soundtrack meets vintage wartime footage. (*Riva / 20ᵗʰ Century*)

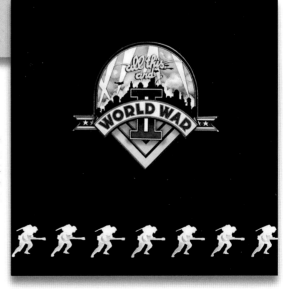

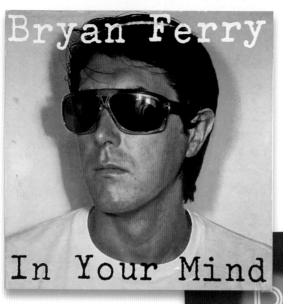

Left: Ferry's first post-split solo record left a lot of people wishing… well, listen and you'll find out. (*EG*)

Right: 1977 brought a second series of *Rock Follies*, and the second soundtrack album wasn't far away. (*Polydor*)

Left: 'A key document in the ongoing development of ambient music…' (*Sky*)

Right: 801's first studio album lacked Eno, but added Godley & Creme. (*Polydor*)

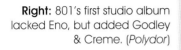

Left: Unreleased until 2001, but a reasonable successor to 801's last live album. (*Expression*)

ROXY MUSIC

I
VIRGINIA PLAIN
DO THE STRAND
ALL I WANT IS YOU
OUT OF THE BLUE
PYJAMARAMA
EDITIONS OF YOU

GREATEST HITS

Right: With the punks hailing Roxy among the past's few worthy heroes, here was a quick compilation to prove them correct. (*Atco*)

Left: *Before and After Science.* The last of Eno's overtly song-driven albums… the future starts here. (*Polydor*)

Right: The reviews for this album were mostly critical. The reviews were wrong. (*EG*)

Left: 'It sounds just great… Whether it goes anywhere is another matter.' (*Trouser Press*). (*EG*)

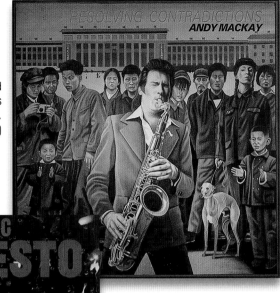

Right: Andy Mackay's second album, released just months before Roxy reconvened. (*Bronze*)

Left: Four years after the siren sang, Roxy were back with a fresh *Manifesto*. (*EG / Polydor / Atco*)

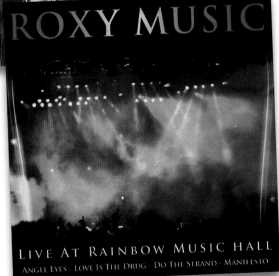

Right: One of a multitude of CD releases for a very singular 1979 live show.

Left: Rock Follies - l-r Charlotte Cornwell, Julie Covington, Rula Lenska.

Right: The original 801 line-up.

Bill MacCormick   Lloyd Watson   Simon Phillips
Brian Eno   Francis Monkman   Phil Manzanera

801 *Live*

E.G. GROUP OF COMPANIES
63A KINGS ROAD, LONDON, SW3 4NT
TEL. 01-730 2161

Left: Phil Manzanera wears his art on his heart.

Session Produced by Tony Wilson
Session Recorded Langham 1, 26 February 1974
Single produced by Eno
Single recorded January 1974
Top Gear Tracks: 'The Paw Paw Negro Blowtorch', 'Baby's On Fire/Totalled', 'Fever'

The UK tour was cancelled on the spot; a proposed European outing likewise. And while the single release went ahead, nobody had their hearts in it any longer. 'Seven Deadly Finns' (and its *Pussyfooting* portion for a B-side) was cursed with minimal airplay and promotion, and wasn't even considered for an already-scheduled John Peel session. Instead, two songs from *Here Come The Warm Jets* were joined by 'Fever' and the otherwise unheard 'Totalled', and the energies of the abandoned tour shone through every second.

As for the single 'Seven Deadly Finns', it remains one of the most left-field loopy outposts in a career that has since redefined such terms – a tongue-twisting tale of seamy seaside sexuality, with French girls wishing someone would make them daisy chains, titular Finns descending like rain, kittens in trees and flirts in print skirts. All offset by the sound of Eno yodelling.

Chapter Six: Destiny Will Stand Corrected

May 1974: Bryan Ferry – 'The 'In' Crowd' b/w 'Chance Meeting (Single)

Personnel: see Another Time, Another Place (below)
Produced by Bryan Ferry, John Punter
Recorded spring 1974
Release date May 1974
Highest chart positions UK: 13, US: did not chart

Interviewed during the sessions for his second solo album, Bryan Ferry told *Melody Maker* how much he'd enjoyed working with Davy O'List back in Roxy's early days and that he hoped to have the opportunity to do so again. O'List was on the phone as soon as he read the article: 'I just called and said, 'Come on then, here I am'. Bryan turned around and said he had just the track for me to play on – a version of 'The 'In' Crowd' – and that's what happened'. (The pair also recorded a new version of 'Sea Breezes': one of the songs O'List had been playing during his tenure with Roxy Music.)

Ferry's instinct was correct. Like the song, O'List's riff is swaggering and arrogant; the sound of drawn flick-knives in the grip of the leering dandy who delivers the lyric. Ferry has never sounded so sure of himself (and that's saying something), and when he remarks almost offhand, 'If it's square, we ain't there', you know that *you* should not be, either.

1 June 1974: Eno – Rainbow Theatre, London

Personnel:
Brian Eno: vocals, synth
Kevin Ayers: John Cale, Archie Legget: bass
Ollie Halsall: guitar
Eddie Sparrow: drums
Robert Wyatt: percussion
Tracks: 'Baby's On Fire', 'Driving Me Backwards'

He might not have been interested in touring, but Eno was all over the record racks during 1974. Credited under his full, 14-syllable name, his contributions are both unmistakable and all-but-indistinguishable across former Hawkwind frontman Robert Calvert's debut solo album *Captain Lockheed and the Starfighters*.

Alongside Phil Manzanera, Eno was in the studio with John Cale for the Welshman's *Fear* album and with fellow ex-Velvet Undergrounder Nico on her *The End*.

Eno was working again with The Portsmouth Sinfonia, rehearsing for their most prestigious gig yet – at the Royal Albert Hall on 28 May – which in turn would be recorded for the *Hallelujah* live album: another Eno production.

He supplied 'Enossification' to Genesis' in-progress *The Lamb Lies Down on Broadway* – a term that left many purchasers with absolutely no idea what they needed to listen out for, but you knew it when you heard it.

But most impressively of all, Eno overcame his aversion to solo live performance sufficiently to appear at one of the most enthralling concerts of the year, as preserved on the now deservedly legendary *June 1, 1974* album.

Cale, Nico and Kevin Ayers would be appearing alongside Eno at an event conceived by one-time *Melody Maker* journalist and now Island A&R man Richard Williams, who had brought both Ayers and Cale to the label. From there, it was simply a matter of convincing them to stage what amounted to a return to the revues of the 1960s past – the days when visiting Motown and Stax packages would hit the stage: four or five headlining singers in one room and a single tight band backing them all. *That* was the spirit that Williams wanted to restore. That was the spirit of the show.

'John (Cale) thought the concert would be good for me', Nico said of her role in the affair some seven years later. 'We had completed (*The End*), and Island wanted to publicise us all. The concert was a way of giving us all equal publicity without having to make us play four separate concerts'. However, it was not a joyous occasion. Nico biographer Richard Witts quotes her as later lamenting, 'It was not four people working together, it was four people fighting for the spotlight. I don't know who was more arrogant. I had the impression that nobody cared. It was a sign of the time. A kind of death wish'.

Witts quotes Eno, too, in equally dismissive mood, although less of the working environment than the media response to the event's very existence. 'There wasn't much really happening' in the rock scene in general, said Eno, 'and, since there are a lot of people who are professionally committed to discovering novelty, this was seized upon and blown up beyond its real significance'. But *Creem* journalist Richard Cromelin speaks for all who either witnessed the show firsthand or were entranced by the resultant live LP. 'Culturally, (*June 1, 1974*) was analogous to a major Dada exhibition back in its heyday; the Academy, in peril, will ignore or scoff, but time will inevitably mould it into an event...'.

For Eno, the opportunity to work with both Cale and Nico was one that he had already embraced, when he joined them in the studio for their latest albums. Maybe he was or maybe he wasn't responsible for the claim that 'not many people heard the Velvets, but everyone who did, formed a band', but his admiration for all they had achieved was all-consuming. He already knew what to expect, of course, from the studio sessions. 'Working with them was of course, interesting; both of them are very demanding people in a way, and so am I in another way'. Cale's drug intake ('I was pretty incorrigible... (Eno would) throw up his arms and say 'Good God' quite a lot') added to the pressures. But Eno was not discouraged. 'It was a very volatile situation, and those are the ones that interest me in music. We weren't sitting around patting each other on the back saying, 'Groovy, let's blow together'. It was quite intense'.

Eno was actually in a more difficult situation than his *bandmates*, as it became clear that he had also been elected the logistical adviser for the entire concert. He told writer Lisa Robinson:

> We decided what the format of the concert would be, and then the role sort of fell on me to be the keeper of the thing. I generally kept it from straying off the subject, which was that somebody would come onstage and then go off again, and then somebody else would have to come on; just the mechanics of what would we do in between the two people; just making sure that we thought about those details of the actual stage problems and the whole layout of the set. So, in fact, the rehearsals were the most efficient rehearsals I've ever been involved in, and we only rehearsed for about 20 or 25 hours at the most, which isn't a lot.

Which, surprisingly, sat well with Ayers as well. As the only headliner on the stage for whom touring was a way of life, he later admitted he expected everyone to be going to him with their questions and problems. Instead, Eno absorbed all the queries, leaving Ayers and his newly named Soporifics backing band to rehearse as much as they felt necessary, then watching the proceedings from the sidelines. Ayers even found time to work alongside Eno and Robert Wyatt on an album with 'Lady' June Cramer: hiking off to David Vorhaus' Kaleiphon Studios in Camden whenever he sensed the opportunity.

Guests were recruited for the concert. Rumour, doubtless in cahoots with a boatload of wishful thinking from sources unknown, suggested that two further former Velvets – guitarist Sterling Morrison and drummer Mo Tucker – had been approached to perform and might have accepted had there been more than a single show on offer. That may or may not be true. 'If there was an offer, I don't remember it, and Maureen has never mentioned it either', Morrison recalled. Which also scotches two other oddly-pervasive legends – that a full Velvets reunion was on the cards, with Eno replacing Lou Reed (!), and that the only reason it *didn't* happen was because the headlining Ayers put his foot down. Guest artists sharing his bill were one thing. Guest legends were something else entirely.

But Robert Wyatt would be making his first public appearance since the accident which left him with a broken back, and Mike Oldfield would turn in only his second since *Tubular Bells* established him as a superstar. (Both appeared during Ayers' set.) And in lieu of some mythical Velvets revamp, Ayers' own newly-formed Soporifics (Ollie Halsall, Archie Legget and John Bundrick) were drafted into Eno and Cale's backing bands. Keyboard player Bundrick recalls:

I knew Eno from my days at Island Records with Free, and all the extra session work I was doing there. The rest of the (Soporifics) I didn't know at the time, but all involved turned out to be absolutely brilliant musicians and brilliant people to hang with. Then, there was also Richard Williams, who I knew really well. I did so many sessions at Island Records, I am so proud that I got to come all the way from Texas, and wind up playing with all these fab musicians in England.

Logistics kept the performances short. Cale would perform three songs; Nico and Eno, two apiece. However, Eno would also perform an encore repeat of 'Baby's On Fire' at the end of the show, while he remained on stage for both Cale and Nico's entire performances. Side one of the *June 1, 1974* album is, effectively, devoted to Eno's work, and both LP and show were generally lauded by the critics. Despite that, the venture was never repeated. Advertising indicated that shows were scheduled for Birmingham and Manchester at the end of June, but they didn't happen.

Island Records suggested staging another full-cast performance at Ayers' upcoming free Hyde Park concert, but Cale dropped out, and Eno had to withdraw after contracting a cold. The following January, Cale suggested that Carnegie Hall had been booked for a show of its own, but nothing came of that either.

However, Eno and Ayers reunited for a Capital Radio session in August, performing (among others) what memory insists was a remarkable piano duet, while Cale, Nico and Eno all reconvened for what is now a semi-legendary performance at the Nationalgalerie in Berlin on 5 October. Ostensibly a Nico headliner, with Cale performing a short set of his own amidships, and Eno contributing electronic shrieks, squeaks and atmospheres throughout, it was always going to be a dramatic evening. The audience response only amplified the drama.

A tape of the show circulates, and it is little short of chaos. The crowd is howling, yelling and complaining throughout, to the point where Eno himself is barely (if at all) audible until Nico's rendition of 'Das Lied Der Deutschen' ('Deutschland Uber Alles') that is itself rendered a distant mumble beneath the audience's caterwauling. But the much-circulated legend that this particular song almost instigated a riot, is clearly exaggerated. There is a lot of booing and yowling, but it's 'Innocent And Vain', oddly, that really gets the crowd going, and it's Eno's (admittedly increasingly irritating) electronic effects that are the principle target of their wrath. By the time Nico gets 'round to the version of 'The End' that closes the concert, the crowd is almost behaving itself.

It was during this same trip, incidentally, that Eno travelled to Hamburg to meet the German band Harmonia; joining them onstage and igniting the partnership that was born with the album *Fabrik, Hamburg*.

July 1974: Bryan Ferry – Another Time Another Place (Album)

Personnel:
Bryan Ferry: vocals, keyboards, harmonica, organ
John Porter: guitar
John Wetton: bass
Paul Thompson: drums
Soloists:
Henry Lowther: trumpet
Chris Mercer: tenor sax
Davy O'List: guitar
Ruan O'Lochlann: alto sax
Chris Pyne: trombone
Vicki Brown, Helen Chappelle, Barry St. John, Liza Strike: backing vocals

Also featuring: Tony Carr, Tony Charles, Alan Skidmore, Alf Reece, Bob Efford, Jeff Daly, Don Cirlio, Bruce Rowland, Morris Pert, Paul Cosh, Martin Drover, Peter Robinson, Ronnie Ross, Steve Saunders, Winston Stone
Produced by Bryan Ferry, John Punter
Recorded spring 1974
Release date 5 July 1974
Highest chart positions. UK: 4, US: did not chart

Tracks: 'The 'In' Crowd', 'Smoke Gets In Your Eyes', 'Walk A Mile In My Shoes', 'Funny How Time Slips Away', 'You Are My Sunshine', '(What A) Wonderful World', 'It Ain't Me Babe', 'Fingerpoppin''/'Help Me Make It Through The Night', 'Another Time, Another Place'

'It seems a pity not to do another solo', Bryan Ferry mused when he was asked if he intended following up *These Foolish Things*. 'There are thousands of other songs I'd like to have a crack at destroying'.

Like its predecessor, *Another Time Another Place* would be built around covers. There was one Ferry original on board – a title track that could easily have dignified *Stranded*, but which certainly made more sense here, closing things out by rounding up the manifold moods and momentum of all that had gone before.

Ferry was now fronting what can only be described as a crack team of session men. Among them ex-Mogul Thrash/Family/King Crimson bassist John Wetton, and former Gonzalez and Keef Hartley Band saxman Chris Mercer, as well as a clutch of familiar faces. The songs themselves fell from even broader branches than last time while rounding up numbers that Ferry, perhaps, would not have dared approach the first time around. The old Platters hit 'Smoke Gets In Your Eyes' was best known in 1974 as the theme to an Esso Blue paraffin commercial: 'I, of course, reply; with lower grades one buys, smoke gets in your eyes'. And while Sam Cooke's '(What A) Wonderful World' and Kris Kristofferson's 'Help Me Make It Through The Night' were standard fare for any number of singers, who but Ferry would have even considered recording 'You Are My Sunshine' and then redefining it around a backdrop of dark clouds and rainstorms?

In terms of arrangement and attitude, *Another Time, Another Place* feels a lot more calculated than *These Foolish Things*. But that itself was surely calculated – the performances that make up the new album are no less exquisitely in tune with the sleeve's glamour-shot cover than *These*

Foolish Things was certainly the work of the black t-shirt-clad thug who gazes menacingly from its front cover.

Indeed, it was with this album and the attendant cover image of an immaculately groomed Ferry standing by a swimming pool that the *New Musical Express* embarked on one of the most inconsequential but hilariously funny campaigns of the age: to rename Bryan Ferry with increasing daftness at every available opportunity. Brown Furry, Brain Fury, El Ferrari… the aliases fell like rain. But while journalist Nick Kent later dismissed the entire affair as 'childish', one cannot help feeling that Ferry enjoyed it; that it pushed him towards further sartorial extremes, just to see what the paper would come up with in reply.

16 July 1974: Andy Mackay - John Peel Show
Personnel
Andy Mackay (sax, clarinet)
plus others
Produced by John Walters
Recorded: Studio T1, Shepherds Bush, 24 June 1974
Tracks: 'The Hour Before', 'Ride Of The Valkyries', 'Walking The Whippet"
August 1974: Andy Mackay – Ride Of The Valkyries' b/w 'Time Regained' (Single) / August

1974: Andy Mackay – In Search Of Eddie Riff (Album)
Personnel:
Andy Mackay: sax, oboe, vocals)
Phil Manzanera: guitar, sax treatment
Lloyd Watson: slide guitar, guitar
John Porter: guitar, bass
Roger Glover: bass
Eddie Jobson: keyboards, synth, glockenspiel, violin, strings and arrangements
Brian Chatton: piano
Paul Thompson: percussion
Bruce Rowlands: percussion
'Countess' Sadie MacKenzie: ethereal voice
Produced by Andy Mackay
Recorded Island Studios, February 1974
Released August 1974
Highest chart positions: did not chart
Tracks (1974 release): 'Wild Weekend', 'The End Of The World', 'Walking The

Whippet', 'What Becomes Of The Brokenhearted', 'An Die Musik', 'Time Regained', 'The Hour Before Dawn', 'Pyramid Of Night', 'The Long And Winding Road', 'Ride Of The Valkyries', 'Summer Sun', 'A Four Legged Friend'
Tracks (1976 release): 'Wild Weekend', 'The End Of The World', 'Walking The Whippet', 'What Becomes Of The Brokenhearted', 'An Die Musik'. 'Time Regained', 'The Hour Before Dawn', 'Pyramid Of Night', 'The Long And Winding Road', 'Ride Of The Valkyries',
1999 bonus tracks (BBC session live rehearsals): 'Ride Of The Valkyries', 'The Hour Before Dawn', 'Walking The Whippet'
Additional tracks personnel" Brian Eno, Jane Riff
Additional tracks Produced by Andy Mackay
Additional Tracks Recorded 1975
Released 1976
Highest chart positions: did not chart

In Search of Eddie Riff came from a desire to play some relatively uncomplicated saxophone with friends', Mackay says in the liner notes for the album's 1999 CD reissue. 'I acknowledged my love of classical music, Motown, '50s rock and roll instrumentals, film music, electronic effects'. He nodded towards his wife Jane's love of country. (Jane died in 1992; the reissue was dedicated to her.) 'I tried singing, I wrote some tunes'. The whole thing was very lighthearted, very easy to listen to, and maybe that's what contributed to the vague sense of disappointment that attended its release.

Not that the album, taken on its own merits, merited any such response. And if there was nothing here as gorgeous as 'A Song For Europe', neither was there anything as off-kilter as 'The Numberer'. Take those two past Mackay compositions as the outer limits, and *In Search Of Eddie Riff* falls effortlessly in between. 'I was trying in a fairly extravagant fashion to find a few musical directions', he told *New Musical Express* scribe Chrissie Hynde (Yes, *that* Chrissie Hynde): 'I didn't go into the studio with any very firm concepts of a particular album. The only kind of unity the album had, was that it was based around a personality which was not my own personality, but an *Eddie Riff* personality which was just a slight shift away from my own'.

There were few surprises among the accompanying musicians, as the rest of Roxy (minus Ferry but plus Eno, who co-wrote 'Time Regained' with Mackay) all threw in. Fairport Convention's Bruce Rowland stepped over from Ferry's last solo sessions; John Porter, as always, proved as majestic on bass as he did on production. Yes, we probably could've lived without another version of 'The Long And Winding Road', but the album's march from pure pop ('What Becomes Of The Brokenhearted') to glam-infused classical (Wagner's 'Ride Of The Valkyries; 'Schubert's 'An Die Musik') is nevertheless as vibrant and vast as it ought to be, while 'Walking The Whippet' (one of five Mackay originals) is 1960s R&B through-and-through. 'In a way, the album is complementary to the Roxy thing', Mackay continued in that *New Musical Express* interview:

> One of the strong elements of Roxy is *style*, I think, particularly on Stranded. It's a kind of cynicism and a replacement of emotion with style – very much Bryan's way of approaching things, in that he couples direct feeling with a stylistic thing – the words and the references and music. Which is, after all, very much what Roxy Music is. And so, some of the approaches to what I did… were the opposite of the way I do things in Roxy.

A second single from the album – 'Wild Weekend' b/w 'Walking The Whippet' – would be released later in the year. The three-CD bonus tracks – described as 'live rehearsals for a BBC *In Concert* broadcast' (which never happened) – are more likely to be a mislabeled release for Mackay's 16 July 1974 Peel session.

October 1974: Roxy Music – 'All I Want Is You' b/w 'Your Application's Failed' (Single) / November 1974: Roxy Music – Country Life (Album)

Personnel:

Bryan Ferry: vocals, keyboards

Andy Mackay: sax

Phil Manzanera: guitar

John Gustafson: bass

Eddie Jobson: keyboards, synthesizer

Paul Thompson: drums

Produced by John Punter/Roxy Music

Recorded AIR Studios, London, July-August 1974

LP Release date 15 November 1974

LP Highest chart positions: UK 3/US 37

Single Release date: October 1974

Single Highest Chart Positions: UK: 12, US: did not chart

Tracks: 'The Thrill Of It All', 'Three And Nine', 'All I Want Is You', 'Out Of The Blue', 'If It Takes All Night', 'Bitter-Sweet', 'Triptych', 'Casanova', 'A Really Good Time', 'Prairie Rose'

By 1974, Roxy Music were sounding tired. No, not tired. Not even a little sleepy. But, where they had once streaked streets ahead of anything that might be described as the competition, suddenly people were catching up. So maybe it wasn't that Roxy Music were moving backwards, but it was the mainstream itself that had stepped forwards. Cockney Rebel and Be-Bop Deluxe – two bands over whom Roxy Music's influence loomed large – were poised to break through at this time; Sparks – whose first hits fell earlier in the year, and who were now onto their second LP of 1974 – not only shared many of Roxy's musical sensibilities, but shared the same record label too. And then there was Queen – still a far cry from the semi-metal monster they would eventually become, but already allying tongue-in-cheek bombast with equally self-deprecating preposterousness, in a manner which could not help but acknowledge Roxy Music's influence.

If ever Roxy Music needed something to remind the kids who the boss really was, it was now. And they did it. Enshrined by Manzanera as 'our best single since 'Virginia Plain'', 'All I Want Is You' could be described as what a sentimental love song would sound like if the Four Horsemen of the Apocalypse formed a band. It's not one of Ferry's cleverest lyrics; rather, it's a list of all the things he doesn't like as much as 'you'. But the record itself is breakneck excitement – spread-eagled sonics that so rush through their allotted time span, that the single feels half the length that it really is. No less than 'Virginia Plain', 'All I Want is You' is one of those records that is gone so quickly that you have no choice: you have to play it again. And again. And again, and then watch the *Top of the Pops* performance, just to embrace the sight of Ferry in t-shirt and jeans, with his thumbs hooked into his pocket tops. Who's the lounge lizard now?

The single's mercurial temperament did not end there either. The Paul Thompson-composed B-side is a jazz funk instrumental into which Manzanera unleashes the kind of wild guitar that we thought maybe Roxy had put to one side. Instead, he was simply laying the groundwork for what was to follow the moment the stylus hit the vinyl of the group's fourth LP.

One of two tracks co-written by Ferry and Manzanera, 'Out Of The Blue' is a showcase for all involved – irrepressible excitement wrapped around some of Manzanera's greatest guitar playing yet. Twenty years later, the song would appear on a various-artists space rock collection – *Space Daze*

2000 – alongside Hawkwind, Fripp & Eno, Kraftwerk, Bowie and more. It didn't sound an inch out of place.

Mackay, too, excelled, co-writing the brooding 'Bitter-Sweet' – 'Song For Europe' revisited in some ways, but so much darker, martial and menacing. And when Ferry digs out the Berlitz phrase book, it's to let rip such a vituperative-sounding stream of German that it was almost inevitable that Roxy's next concert stage set should put some viewers in mind of the Nuremberg Rallies. Or not, as Chris Salewicz argued in the *New Musical Express* at the time:

> We must accept, I think, that in no way did Bry' contemplate any possible ambivalence in the backcloth's giant eagle and its Roxy Music logo and the six red pendants – three on either side of the stages – hanging ceremoniously from the top of the proscenium arch to just above the stage. And with that tidily earmarked, we can dismiss any nasty little memories of the Third Reich that Ferry's strongly disciplinarian onstage outfit might bring to mind, and just get to mental grips with the idea of the army shirt, Sam Browne belt, jodphurs and boots being not an expression of any Adolf Hitler admiration, but just a replacement for the foolhardy image of the Pancho Villa of the Odeon Pampas by a slightly more in-character Douglas Fairbanks of the Yukon.

The other song that raises *Country Life* to its most vaulted height, is 'Casanova' – a savage put-down of an unnamed rival, that is so exquisitely detailed that Ferry must've had somebody very specific in mind ('I know my place is here with you tonight, but not together'). Neither did the animosity fade: two years later, he revisited the song for one of his solo career's B-side Roxy covers.

With these in mind, it's not difficult to understand how the *New Musical Express'* Nick Kent was so effusive in his praise for *Country Life*: 'I'm not even going to start bothering on about this being one of the best albums of the year, and Roxy being a good country mile (sic) ahead of the Bowies, Reeds and Sparks of this world'. Kent referred to Ferry as 'the most important songwriter so far to grace the '70s'. But even Kent conceded that Roxy needed to 'loosen up', because 'mannerisms (are) only useful for so long'. Kent was also unclear about precisely what was happening when the stylus reached 'Triptych' – 'a short bout of ersatz Olde-English pageantry... which is very strange, and in the final analysis, should have been left to the likes of Steeleye Span'.

If *Country Life* has one all-pervading quality, it is weariness – not in terms of its songs, its delivery or its energy levels, but on a deeper plain: the sense that the experiment with which the band was at its outset so enamoured, had reached its end; that hereon out (and maybe for a short while beforehand), they have said all they ever intended saying, and are now simply repeating themselves in different voices. The *New Musical Express*' Max Bell put that very idea to Manzanera at the time, specifically asking whether Roxy had 'reached some kind of pinnacle whereby they're excellent without being startling?' Manzanera responded:

I hope not, though I see what you mean. *Country Life* was really a continuation of *Stranded*. The difficulty is that to do something good and different, there has to be an element of group compromise. In the past, I've had ideas and left them because you're working within a limited framework. That's the whole purpose of doing a solo album. The way we write involves a lot of homework rather than coming in with the completed material. It's a better system, but you're still bound to get a failure rate.

Nowhere was this sense of familiarity more pronounced than in the choice of cover art. From the outset, Roxy artwork had owed as much to pin-up sensibilities as to album sleeve tradition – from the 1950s innocence of the first LP's Kari-Ann, to the more brooding sheen of Amanda Lear on *For Your Pleasure*, and on to the centrefold sensibilities of Marilyn Cole's *Stranded*. (Though fully dressed on the album, Cole herself was the first full-frontal nude centrefold in *Playboy*'s history and was Playmate of the Year for 1973.)

Now, the gloves – and other things – were off. Two young ladies guard the frond-filled gateway to *Country Life*. One stands topless with her hands covering her nipples, her genitalia only scantily concealed by her near-transparent knickers. The other wears a bra that makes no secret of her nipples, while the hand that lies between her legs does not look as though it is simply covering things up.

Ferry dismissed the controversy by explaining the joke. It didn't really work. He told *Circus*: 'It's like the total antithesis of what a real *Country Life* magazine cover would be. *Country Life* is the most traditionally English of magazines. I used their typeface for our name, but I couldn't say 'Country Life' in *their* face, so the album title is in the old 'Roxy Music' script from our first album'.

The problem was... well, look at it! Far-more-revealing album covers had shocked the shockable in the past, but somehow, even the barest of them all – John and Yoko's all-nude *Wedding Album;* Hendrix's naked-breasted *Electric Ladyland* – felt as though they were mere exercises in titillation. *Country Life,* on the other hand, was borderline pornographic.

At home, perhaps surprisingly, very little was said – the general response being little more than a tutted 'Boys will be boys will be boy-oy-oys', as Ferry himself once put it. In the USA, however, the reaction was so outraged that initial pressings of the album were hastily encased in green plastic shrink-wrap before being shipped to the stores, and the sleeve itself was withdrawn the moment that first shipment was complete. The ladies were not even replaced; they were removed altogether, to leave the purchaser staring at nothing more than a clump of bush. One doubts whether that was a deliberate joke. That such attention should be lavished on the American release reminds us just how crucial that country was to Roxy Music's dreams of world domination. And *Country Life* made them a few more friends, particularly after a handful of courageous record store owners succeeded in importing copies of the uncensored album jacket.

More photos appeared in more magazines; more songs on more FM radio stations. The group's first American label – Warner Bros. – released a single of 'Do the Strand' b/w 'Virginia Plain' in the Back to Back Hits series; their then-current label Atlantic hit back with 'If It Takes All Night'. Suddenly, Roxy Music were hot.

They would be back in the US in February 1975, and this time they'd be going for the throat. In the meantime, there was another UK and European tour to handle.

21-22 September 1974 Capitol Theatre, Cardiff, Wales
23-24 September 1974 Colston Hall, Bristol
27 September 1974 Trentham Gardens, Stoke
28-29 September 1974 Odeon, Birmingham
01 October 1974 De Montford Hall, Leicester
03 October 1974 City Hall, Sheffield
05-08 October 1974 Rainbow Theatre, London
13-14 October 1974 Winter Gardens, Bournemouth
16-17 October 1974 Empire, Liverpool
18 October 1974 Belle Vue, Manchester
19 October 1974 Leeds University, Leeds
21-22 October 1974 Odeon, Edinburgh

23-26 October 1974 Apollo, Glasgow
27-28 October 1974 City Hall, Newcastle
05 November 1974 Waldbühne, Berlin, Germany
08 November 1974 Konserthuset, Stockholm, Sweden
10 November 1974 Olympen, Lund, Sweden
11 November 1974 Scandinavium, Gothenbourg, Sweden
19 November 1974 Philipshalle, Dusseldorf, Germany
21 November 1974 Volkshaus, Zurich, Switzerland
24 November 1974 Voorburg De Vliegermolen Holland
26 November 1974 Ciné Roma, Antwerp, Belgium
27 November 1974 Palais des Congrès, Porte Maillot, France
29 November 1974 The Roxy Theatre, Atlanta, GA

15 February 1975 Irvine Auditorium, Philadelphia, USA
20 February 1975 Orpheum Theatre, Boston, USA
21 February 1975 Academy Of Music NYC, USA
22 February 1975 Fresh Energies Theatre, Homestead, PA, USA
24 February 1975 Ford Auditorium, Detroit, USA
26 February 1975 Riverside Theatre, Milwaukee, USA
27 February 1975 Music Hall, Cleveland, Ohio, USA
01 March 1975 Akron Civic Theater, Akron, USA
03 March 1975 Ford Auditorium, Detroit, USA
07 March 1975 Santa Monica Civic Auditorium, Santa Monica, CA

November 1974: Brian Eno – Taking Tiger Mountain (By Strategy) (Album)
Personnel:
Brian Eno: vocals, guitar, keyboards, effects
Phil Manzanera: guitar
Brian Turrington: bass
Freddie Smith: drums
Robert Wyatt: percussion, backing vocals
The Portsmouth Sinfonia: strings
Randi & the Pyramids, The Simplistics: chorus
Polly Eltes: vocals
Phil Collins: drums
Produced by Eno
Recorded Island Studios, London, September 1974
Release date November 1974

Highest chart positions: did not chart
Tracks: 'Burning Airlines Give You So Much More', 'Back In Judy's Jungle', 'The Fat Lady Of Limbourg', 'Mother Whale Eyeless', 'The Great Pretender', 'Third Uncle', 'Put A Straw Under Baby', 'The True Wheel', 'China My China', 'Taking Tiger Mountain'

If Art Pepper had played jazz saxophone with the same disregard for convention that Eno adopted for songwriting, the entire story of post-war jazz would've taken a turn that we would still be recovering from now. And if Eno had played the game that his label and swathes of the still-loyal Roxy following had hopes for: ditto.

Taking Tiger Mountain is a brilliant record. But it is brilliant on its own terms, with (almost) every song layered with so many tricks and misdirections that almost every fresh hearing unearths something new. The album is littered with hits. The goth band Bauhaus came closest with their take on the pulsating proto-punk 'Third Uncle'; A Certain Ratio took their name from 'The True Wheel'. But anyone who can listen to the album and walk away without at least one chorus burned into their head does not have a soul.

'Put A Straw Under Baby', with The Portsmouth Sinfonia sawing gleefully in the background, Robert Wyatt on treated backing vocals, and a lyric that's a second cousin to some of Hillaire Belloc's more cautionary tales, is irresistibility personified. But so is 'The Fat Lady Of Limbourg': all jellyfish kisses, duck quacks and black eggs, it's a nonsense tale of such epic proportions that it could almost be the Brothers Grimm.

'Burning Airlines Give You So Much More', 'Back In Judy's Jungle'; song after song impales itself on your consciousness until you reach the final opus and what sounds like the Red Army choir steps out to serenade your ascent of Tiger Mountain. Oh, and Phil Collins pops up on 'Mother Whale Eyeless': today, reminding us of a time when his presence helped dignify any album on which he appeared.

Astonishingly, given the album's subsequent renown, early reviews of *Taking Tiger Mountain (By Strategy)* were less than glowing: a development that certainly hastened Eno's quest to determine a fresh musical direction. But he would probably have taken such a turn regardless – other events early in the new year would see to that.

19 December 1974: Bryan Ferry – Live at the Royal Albert Hall, 1974 (Released 2020)

Personnel:
Bryan Ferry: vocals, keyboards

Phil Manzanera: guitar
John Porter: guitar
John Wetton: bass
Mike Moran, Peter Robinson: keyboards
Eddie Jobson: piano, violin
Paul Thompson: drums
Morris Pert: percussion
Jeff Daly: sax
Ronnie Ross, Chris Mercer: sax
Malcolm Griffiths: trombone
Martin Drover, Paul Cosh: trumpet
Doreen Chanter, Helen Cahhelle, Vicki Brown: backing vocals
Tracks: 'Sympathy For The Devil', 'I Love How You Love Me', 'Baby I Don't Care',
'It's My Party', 'Don't Worry Baby', 'Another Time, Another Place', 'Fingerpoppin'',
'The Tracks Of My Tears', 'You Won't See Me', 'Smoke Gets In Your Eyes', 'A
Hard Rain's A-Gonna Fall', 'A Really Good Time', 'The 'In' Crowd', 'These Foolish
Things'

When Bryan Ferry appeared at London's Royal Albert Hall in December
1974, it was the second time of trying. He'd been hoping to play there
back in January, only to be foiled by the establishment's then doggedly-
upheld but ultimately short-lived ban on rock performances. Now,
the powers that be had relented, and two further shows were quickly
slotted in: one at City Hall, Newcastle, on 17 December, and the other
at Birmingham Odeon the following night. All three, of course, would
focus almost wholly on material from his two solo albums to date. Just
one Roxy Music song made it in ('A Real Good Time', naturally), and
just one other self-composed song: the title track from *Another Time,
Another Place*. The remainder of the set focussed on that whirling tour
through the vortex of pop history that spun out of the original LPs.

Philip Norman reviewed the London performance for *The Times*, and
he did not seem to be expecting a pleasant evening: 'The power of
Bryan Ferry is the power of visual anachronism', he wrote. 'It engages
our attention that a man wearing evening dress and hair dressing,
should sway and bend his knees in the execution of a rock song. It
surprises us that a voice little stronger than that of a guards subaltern
on amateur night, should be exercised upon the songs of Brian Wilson,
Kris Kristofferson and Stevie Wonder'. His forebodings, he concluded,
were correct: 'There is seldom pleasure in material regurgitated without

improvement or affection. There is no pleasure in the subjecting of such material to Mr Ferry's self-satisfied parody'.

Other voices, of course, were kinder, if no less bemused. Reviewing the gig for the *New Musical Express*, Max Bell wrote, 'At ten to nine, there's a momentary hush as the lights dim, then a huge roar announces the emergence of the group and orchestra: the former resplendent in tuxedos and looking distinctly self-conscious. But just as you're musing the wisdom of that venture, eyes left while a huge spotlight follows the evening star across the marble. Ferry – formally smart in a dark dinner suit and patent leather hair – swaggers to a centre microphone and introduces himself with 'Sympathy For The Devil''.

Ferry, too, appears to have viewed the evening as something quite out of the ordinary. Looking back on the occasion for the show's 2020 CD release, he agreed, 'It was fun to play these songs from another era – quite different from what I was doing with Roxy – and when we added the orchestra for these shows, it really felt like something special. Accordingly, we dressed in black tie'.

The sheer haste of Roxy's mid-1970s career – and some once-irreparable technical problems – had kept the tapes under wraps back then, and maybe the time had never felt right for any subsequent reappraisal. Forty-six years on, however, *Live at the Royal Albert Hall, 1974* emerged as a glorious time capsule: a 14-song-strong blast that (like his first album) opened with 'Sympathy For The Devil' and closed with 'These Foolish Things'. In between, however, it embraced everything from 'Fingerpoppin'' to 'The Tracks Of My Tears'; rocked out for 'The 'In' Crowd' and 'A Hard Rain's A-Gonna Fall', and reminded us just what courageous releases these two LPs were at the time. Ferry, after all, was widely regarded among the most adventurous songwriters of the era. What the devil was he doing singing 'It's My Party'?

The mix on the finished CD isn't great. While Ferry and the piano are clear as a bell, Phil Manzanera is annoyingly low on the scale, and his bandmates aren't treated much better. The show remains absurdly enjoyable, of course, but one hopes it sounded better on the night.

Chapter Seven: Ha-ha, Isn't Life a Circus?

December 1974: Brian Eno – Christmas Single

According to John Cale, Eno rounded off his 1974 by recording a 'bizarre' Christmas single. It opened with the words 'I can hear the reindeer', and ended with 'Here comes Santa Claus', but who knows what occurred in between? The record was never released.

Eno continued to be busy nevertheless – a workaholic who was scarcely slowed even after he was hit by a taxi on a rainswept Harrow Road on 18 January. Hospitalised, he simply used the time to invent ambient music. Back on his feet by March, he made his way to New York City to produce a set of demos for the band Television (Island were interested in signing them at the time). He oversaw Robert Calvert's latest solo project *Lucky Leif and the Longships*, Robert Wyatt's *Ruth is Stranger than Richard*, and was intimately involved in a jazz rock reinterpretation of *Peter and the Wolf*. According to the credits, Eno played the pond. He again joined Manzanera on a new John Cale album – *Slow Dazzle* – and later in the year was back alongside the Welshman for the follow-up *Helen of Troy*.

And he went out on tour again.

May 1975 saw Eno and Fripp arrange a seven-city European outing, effectively restaging *(No Pussyfooting)* and its newly-completed successor *Evening Star* before a succession of audiences that surely had no idea what to expect. One thing is certain, however: they didn't appreciate what they received. There were no starless schizoid men or fat Limbourgian ladies on display; nobody taking Tiger Mountain or chasing ladies of the road – just a loop of filmmaker Malcolm LeGrice's *Berlin Horse* short, which was the sole illumination for what was happening onstage, which wasn't much: one figure behind a soaring bank of electronics; the other seated, guitar in hand.

The outcome was seldom pretty. In Madrid for the opening night, the duo had barely played for ten minutes before the audience made its irritation known. In Saint Etienne, the pair were booed off stage, and the Paris show was marked by so many disturbances and interruptions that the scheduled second night was cancelled altogether.

The overall dislocation of the evening was subsequently enhanced for non-attendees by the poor-quality audience recording of the show that later emerged. It was this tape that was restored to something approaching a listenable (but still crowd-heavy) standard for release through Fripp's DGM website and later on CD: where it is appended with an additional 45 minutes worth of Eno's prerecorded tape loops.

April 1975: Phil Manzanera – Diamond Head (Album)
Personnel:
Phil Manzanera: guitar, synth, bass
Robert Wyatt: vocals
Brian Eno: vocals, guitar, piano, treatments
Doreen Chanter: vocals
John Wetton, Brian Turrington: bass
Bill MacCormick: bass, vocals
Eddie Jobson: synth
Dave Jarrett: keyboards
Andy Mackay: sax
Ian MacDonald: bagpipes
Paul Thompson: drums
Charles Hayward, Sonny Akpan: percussion
Produced by Phil Manzanera
Recorded Island Studios, December 1974 – January 1975
Released April 1975
Highest chart positions: did not chart
Tracks: 'Frontera', 'Diamond Head', 'Big Day', 'The Flex', 'Same Time Next Week',
'Miss Shapiro', 'East Of Echo', 'Lagrima', 'Alma
2011 bonus Tracks: 'Carhumba', 'Corazon Y Alma

September 1975: Quiet Sun – Mainstream (Island HELP 19)
Personnel:
Phil Manzanera: guitar
Bill MacCormick: bass
Charles Hayward: drums
Dave Jarrett: keyboards
Brian Eno: synth
Produced by Quiet Sun
Recorded Island Studios, January 1975
Released September 1975
Highest chart positions: did not chart
Tracks: 'Sol Caliente', 'Trumpet With Motherhood', 'Bargain Classics', 'R. F. D.',
'Mummy Was An Asteroid...', 'Trot', 'Rongwrong'
Collectors Edition Bonus Tracks: 'Years Of The Quiet Sun', 'Trot' (Original demo),
'R.F.D.' (Warner Bros. demo), 'R.F.D. Part 1' (Mainstream session), 'Talking History
(Interviews)'

As Phil Manzanera prepared to release his first solo album, the irony of Roxy Music's recent history was inescapable. The guitarist told *Sounds'* Pete Makowski:

> Since *Stranded,* there will have been five albums from the band and separate members. If we had come to that kind of understanding before (Eno quit), it may have solved things. But we were heading up so fast that everything was happening. The way it is at the moment, we've hardly done any touring, and that's left large gaps where people have got up and done their own thing. I think we've all benefitted from these things, and our (new) album – which we're three-quarters through now – will show how it's benefitted.

Later in life, Manzanera still looked back upon that period between *Stranded* (1973) and *Siren* (1975), with something approaching astonishment:

> It was like we were a bunch of maniacs let loose. Once somebody said, 'You've got a recording contract', everyone said, 'Right, well, I've got 50 million other things I want to do apart from my stuff with you lot', so we'd do a Roxy album, and at the same time I'd be working on my solo album, on Eno's solo albums once he got the boot; other people. It was wonderful! I'd been waiting for years for this opportunity to be a professional musician, and suddenly somebody gave me the green light. In the '70s, the nature of the business was slightly different, in that you could go to the record company and say, 'I've got this project; it's not commercial at all', and they'd say, 'Here's a budget, go away and do it'. And it didn't matter if it was a huge seller or not because the pressure wasn't on the company like it is today.

He also acknowledges Island Records' part in the process: 'I was very lucky to be with Island, Chris Blackwell, the whole spirit. The independent labels had started – Virgin, Chrysalis, Island – and they were the real unique pioneers of British music in terms of the industry. They had a wider musical vision than the majors at that time, so a lot of interesting things came out on those labels'.

Taking full advantage of this freedom, Manzanera was in many ways now the most visible current member of Roxy Music. His work with Eno on *Here Come The Warm Jets,* and as co-producer on *Taking Tiger*

Mountain (By Strategy), was followed swiftly by engagements alongside John Cale and Nico.

Now, aside from his own first solo album *Diamond Head* (which featured contributions from Eno, Thompson, Mackay, Jobson, and the latest Roxy Music bassist: John Wetton), Manzanera was also reconvening his pre-Roxy Music band Quiet Sun for the album *Mainstream*, to make the album that their original demo tapes had promised they might. 'I was told I could do a solo album', Manzanera recalled. 'So I went off to Basing Street Studios and booked it from 12 to 12, and everyone said fine. From 12 to 6, I did *Diamond Head*; from 6 to 12, I did Quiet Sun; I didn't tell Island, and then I presented them with two albums'.

Incidentally, a mark of the speed with which the two records were recorded, can be found by consulting Manzanera's engagement diary for early-1975. Roxy Music's February-1975 tour of North America was set to begin in a little under four weeks (26 days, to be precise); the final mix for Quiet Sun was completed in one final all-night session immediately before he left for Toronto.

Diamond Head appeared first, and there were few surprises in the personnel department. Robert Wyatt was invited in to voice a song that he and Manzanera had already recorded for Wyatt's second solo set: 'Team Spirit' was retitled 'Frontera', and actively emerged a far better beast. Eno introduced seething eccentricity to the insanely poppy 'Big Day': a Peruvian holiday postcard in which he even agrees to 'retail crummy cosmetics' if he can only afford to return there. He then proceeded to outdo even that with 'Miss Shapiro': a song that is simultaneously so *out there*, that it all but meets itself coming in through the main door of *Top Of The Pops*. Irresistible indeed, in those days when Britain was riven by strikes and industrial content, its a-wop-bopping backing vocals croon 'shop-steward, shop-shop steward' while Eno intones breakneck twisting tongue tortures that defy anyone to sing along.

Doreen Chanter duets with John Wetton on 'Same Time Next Week', and Bill MacCormick's performance on his co-write 'Alma' makes one wonder why he didn't exercise his vocal cords more often.

But to dwell on the songs is to disregard the title track: a cut that even made it into Roxy Music's live set; the soaring 'The Flex'; the aching duet for guitar and oboe that is the hauntingly brief 'Lagrima', and a phased and fuzzing introduction to Quiet Sun: one of two full bands that roar through 'East Of Echo'. A live outing for the whole affair could not be far away... could it?

Two bonus tracks were attached to the 2011 remaster – 'Carhumba' (also present on the album's 1999 reissue) was recorded with South African trumpeter Mongezi Feza (most recently sighted alongside Robert Wyatt), and the ten-minute 'Corazon Y Alma' dated back to 1971 and Quiet Sun's demos. Sharp ears might well spot how this was then sliced up to create no less than *four* of the solo album's songs – 'Lagrima', 'Frontera', 'East Of Echo' and 'Alma' – hence its appearance here and not among the bonus tracks on the same year's Quiet Sun anthology.

The fruits of the Quiet Sun sessions emerged in September on Island's budget-priced HELP line. Bill MacCormick had again drifted out of music, instead studying for extra A-Levels before moving on to the London School of Economics to read politics: 'I had a place there, and at Warwick. I really hadn't played bass for some months when Phil explained his plan, so I started some desperate practicing'. Rehearsals were few and far between; Manzanera later revealed the musicians had time for just two rehearsals before the tapes started rolling. MacCormick agrees:

First takes were the norm, and I don't think any of us expected it to come out the way it did. Obviously, Phil had a lot more studio experience, and Rhett Davis as engineer made an enormous difference. John Wetton helped me by lending me a lovely Fender Precision. We got rid of some of the more meandering pieces, and with 'Corazon Y Alma' being used on *Diamond Head* in various ways, we basically did everything that was left over, and really just tried to enjoy ourselves. We all knew it was a one-off; no careers were on the line. So fun. With added Eno. The way it was recorded, meant we had no time to dwell on things. Just record, do a few overdubs and mix. As I said, a lot of things were first takes, and that includes my personal favorite of anything I ever played, which is the bass solo on 'Rongwrong'.

MacCormick continues: 'Recording two albums in the time allocated to make one was an inspired decision by Phil. Neither his management nor his record company knew anything about it. I suspect Quiet Sun probably got better reviews than *Diamond Head*'.

For Manzanera, the irony was the memory of those hapless days before he joined Roxy Music: 'I'd gone around with Quiet Sun demos, and everyone told me 'Forget it, you'll never get a deal with that stuff'. It had zero commercial potential, so this was my way of getting back at them'. Island was one of the labels who turned it down, 'So, ironically and perversely, they were now being forced to release it. And it was *Melody Maker*'s Record of the Month. It didn't sell anything, but me and the rest of the guys in Quiet Sun were able to cock a snook at the industry. I'd kept all the original rejection letters as well, so I was able to go back in with the letters and the *Melody Maker* review and say, 'Look, you've just released the album you turned down!'.

Mainstream was indeed a revelation. It remained, sonically and stoically, very much a child of its original time: that is, the early-1970s. One could also say that MacCormick's subsequent work with Matching Mole had defused some of the more *outre* elements of the original Quiet Sun sound, just as time and a general broadening of musical horizons had lessened the extremes that Quiet Sun had allegedly been prone to reach. And so, *Mainstream* slipped seamlessly into the mid-1970s; a brittle excursion that – while it certainly picked up where Soft Machine and the Mole left off – carried its threads in a totally different direction: to a point, one might tentatively venture, where titles like 'Sol Caliente' and Hayward's vocal excursion 'Rongwrong' could've passed as having skittered out of one of David Bowie's notebooks.

Meanwhile, MacCormick's 'Mummy Was An Asteroid, Daddy Was A Small Non-Stick Kitchen Utensil' overcame even the insanity of both its eventual title and its earlier incarnation as 'Mummy Was A Maoist, Daddy Was A Running Dog Capitalist Lackey of the Bourgeoisie', to dish up a tour of the entire cosmos in little more than six minutes.

Even more surreal is the memory of Radio One's Anne Nightingale playing it, one afternoon in summer 1975. Oh, how we danced.

July 1975: Bryan Ferry – 'You Go To My Head' b/w 'Re-make/Re-model' (Single)

Personnel (see Let's Stick Together below)
Produced by Bryan Ferry, Chris Thomasr
Recorded 1975
Release date July 1975
Highest chart positions UK: 33, US: did not chart

Originally written in 1938 by Haven Gillespie and the splendidly-named J. Fred Coots, 'You Go To My Head' again found Ferry doing battle with the legends of song. Judy Garland, Frank Sinatra, Fats Waller, Ella Fitzgerald and Bing Crosby rank among those who had recorded it before him. Ferry, however, sounds as comfortable here as he did the last time he walked with such giants (*These Foolish Things*). Even classier, though, is the accompanying video reuniting the now super-stylish tux-clad Ferry with Roxy Music's first LP cover star Kari-Ann; the lyric's air of obsession crystallised not only by her dreamlike appearances and disappearances but also by the picture that hangs on the wall above the fireplace. It's the first Roxy Music album, of course.

August 1975: Brian Eno – 'The Lion Sleeps Tonight' b/w 'I'll Come Running' (Single)

Personnel (A-side):
Brian Eno: vocals, electronics
Philip Rambow, Guy Humphreys: guitar
Brian Turrington: bass
Mike Desmarais: drums
Personnel (B-side): See below
Produced by Eno
Recorded Island Studios, London, July-August 1975
Release date August 1975
Highest chart positions: did not chart

Eno's second solo single was – and might even remain – the most mystifying thing he has ever recorded: a rendering of the 'Wimoweh' classic that is so straight-faced that he had to be laughing all the way through it. Recorded with The Winkies the previous year, it had already spent more than 12 months on the shelf, leading some observers to wonder why he chose to release it now; because the new LP that it accompanied could not have been further removed from it.

August 1975: Brian Eno – Another Green World (Album)

Personnel:
Brian Eno: vocals, guitar, synth
Robert Fripp: guitar
Brian Turrington: bass, piano
Paul Rudolph, Percy Jones: bass
Rod Melvin: keyboards
John Cale: viola
Phil Collins: drums
Produced by Eno

Recorded Island Studios, London, July-August 1975
Release date September 1975
Highest chart positions: did not chart
Tracks: 'Sky Saw', 'Over Fire Island', 'St. Elmo's Fire', 'In Dark Trees', 'The Big Ship', 'I'll Come Running', 'Another Green World', 'Sombre Reptiles', 'Little Fishes', 'Golden Hours', 'Becalmed', 'Zawinul-Lava', 'Everything Merges With The Night', 'Spirits Drifting'

Phil Collins' appearance on *Taking Tiger Mountain* may have been fleeting, but it birthed what the drummer later called 'a beautiful relationship'. As Eno worked on *Another Green World*, the two not only paired up once more – for three tracks this time – but the experience also coalesced Collins' Brand X side-project in his mind, bringing a bunch of people into the studio just to see what happened. What happened on this occasion was – given the ringmaster – typically disorientating. On one occasion, Eno handed everybody present a piece of paper, and told them to make lists from one to 15. He would then assign a note to each number – number two was G, number seven was C#, and so on – and then had them play, simply to find out what it would sound like. Collins described the exercise as 'painting by numbers'. Another time, Eno asked Collins and bassist Percy Jones to run through every lick and riff they knew, so he could cut them up for loops.

John Cale passed through – eerie on the lurching 'Sky Saw' – confirming his later remark that the best thing to come out of *June 1, 1974,* was his friendship with Eno, while Robert Fripp loaned some distinctively-characteristic guitar to a couple of tracks. The bulk of the album however, was Eno alone, stepping far beyond the expectations that his previous two LPs had established.

Oblique Strategies came into play. This was a set of notes he first started making for himself early on in Roxy Music's lifespan: instructions, observations, notions, aphorisms. He kept them for his own amusement and sometimes elucidation, but one day mentioned them to artist Peter Schmidt, and was astonished to learn that he too guided his work by referring to a similar oracle. In 1975, the pair pooled their resources, and published them as a set of cards, which promptly underwent the harshest baptism imaginable: Eno walking into the studio without the remotest idea of what he intended to do, with nothing written or even planned. And, for four days, nothing happened.

But then it did. Perhaps it took Eno that much time to relax into the notion that his instincts clashing with chance could be productive.

Perhaps it took the cards that long to attune themselves to his needs; he did not, after all, call them 'oracle cards' for nothing. Either way, *Another Green World* began unfolding, and Eno gave the deck free rein to take him where it wished.

Aggressive without being angry, edgy without feeling precarious, *Another Green World* did free a few vocals from the album's largely instrumental constraints – the crooning 'St. Elmo's Fire', the ultra-lithe 'I'll Come Running' and the *Taming Tiger Mountain*-topping 'Golden Hours'. But 'In Dark Trees' needed only instrumentation to illustrate its foreboding title; 'Another Green World' and 'The Big Ship' sailed seas of synthesized imagination: as innocently enjoyable as watching robins take a bath in a puddle. 'Little Fishes' swim, bubbling around their pond, and then there's 'Sombre Reptiles' – Peruvian percussion slipping through the undergrowth; Komodo keys droning dragon-like over the echo. Into the last year of Roxy, and the first of Ferry's solo career, that same percussive backdrop would become all-pervading in their music. This might be where it started.

'Sombre Reptiles' was, and remains, one of Eno's finest hours. It was so evocatively titled that it really could not be about anything else. Maybe nobody needs to know that there was even an accompanying dance for it – enacted by pupils of the fifth form at a boarding school in Southern England – which required all participants to steadfastly adopt a reptilian pose and then look sombre, but there was.

Hindsight declares *Another Green World* to have marked a new beginning for Eno, although no one could've predicted what that beginning might be. For now, we were content in declaring that he'd simply fabricated a new kind of pop or – as he explained to *Sounds'* Vivien Goldman – an old form of music:

My first album *Here Come The Warm Jets* is my least favourite. It sold best of all. But a lot of people genuinely prefer it. They heard that under the condition of wanting to like it a lot, and that makes a difference. I prefer... *Another Green World*. It's less aggressive; there's less adolescent banging about. Although there's fast numbers on *Another Green World*, they're much smoother. 'St. Elmo's Fire' is more like a sledge shooting over snow, that kind of speed. I want to make disposable albums. Well, I suppose albums are disposable, but I want to make records to get up with for a couple of weeks because it has a nice sparkle, a nice shimmer to it, and there's no pretence that this is... music.

An Obscure Interlude
Late-1975 – Brian Eno/Obscure Records

Obscure 1: Gavin Bryars – The Sinking Of The Titanic (Album)
Tracks: 'The Sinking Of The Titanic', 'Jesus' Blood Never Failed Me Yet'
Produced by Brian Eno

Obscure 2: Christopher Hobbs/John Adams/Gavin Bryars – Ensemble Pieces (Album)
Tracks: 'Aran' (Hobbs), 'American Standard': 'John Philip Sousa'/'Christian Zeal and Activity'/'Sentimentals' (Adams), 'McCrimmon Will Never Return' (Hobbs), '1, 2, 1-2-3-4' (Bryars)
Produced by Brian Eno

Obscure 3: Brian Eno – Discreet Music (Album)
Tracks: 'Discreet Music', 'Three Variations On The Canon In D Major By Johann Pachelbel: (1) Fullness Of Wind; (2) French Catalogues; (3) Brutal Ardour
Produced by Eno
Recorded home studio May 1975 (a-side), Trident Studios, London September 1975 (b-side)
Release date December 1975
Highest chart positions: did not chart

Obscure 4: David Toop/Max Eastley – New And Rediscovered Musical Instruments (Album)
Tracks: 'Hydrophone' (Eastley), 'Metallophone' (Eastley), 'The Centriphone' (Eastley), 'Elastic Aerophone/Centriphone' (Eastley), 'Do The Bathosphere' (Toop), 'The Divination Of The Bowhead Whale' (Toop), 'The Chairs Story' (Toop)
Produced by Brian Eno

It was at the world premier of Gavin Bryars' *The Sinking of the Titanic* on 11 December 1972 at London's Queen Elizabeth Hall, that Eno was inspired to create his groundbreaking Obscure Records: a label home for experimental composition. Bryars told Culturekiosque.com: '(Eno) actually admires this kind of music, which he first heard as a painting student developing into a rock musician. To him, this music is very accessible while still challenging certain musical conventions. He wanted to produce albums with this sort of music, because he thought the public was being deprived of it'.

Into the new year, with artist Alan Power adding his thoughts to Eno and Bryars' enthusiasm, the idea of a record label slowly fermented. Indeed, Bryars explains: 'The idea for making recordings came initially from Alan Power, who wanted to find a way of releasing recordings of the soundtracks from the various underground films that he'd supported as producer'. Soon the three were meeting with Island Records to discuss the project. Their thoughts were met with enthusiasm, only for the dream to crash against the same oil-crisis/vinyl-shortage arguments that were scotching so many other projects and bands at that time. The idea lay dormant for the next two years.

Then came Eno's road accident. He wrote in his album's liner notes:

In January this year, I had an accident. I was not seriously hurt, but I was confined to bed in a stiff and static position. My friend Judy Nylon visited me and brought me a record of 18th-century harp music. After she had gone – and with some considerable difficulty – I put on the record. Having laid down, I realized that the amplifier was set at an extremely low level, and that one channel of the stereo had failed completely. Since I hadn't the energy to get up and improve matters, the record played on almost inaudibly. This presented what was, for me, a new way of hearing music: as part of the ambience of the environment, just as the colour of the light and the sound of the rain were parts of that ambience.

Music that existed outside of the realms that are traditionally regarded *as* music, has probably always existed, and was certainly a powerful force throughout the 20th century, as a variety of schools and disciplines emerged to chase the concept down different avenues. All are pathways within a wide world of eclecticism, which in turn was generally lumped in beneath the overall banner of experimental music. Around the mid-1970s, however, more specific terms began to coalesce around the work of certain artists. Eno and his Obscure series of album releases played a major role in this.

Veering away from the project's original notions – but bearing in mind the revelation that came to Eno on his sick bed – he and Bryars, together with critic Michael Nyman, were now scheming a label that would offer at least a modicum of mainstream attention to those composers and performers whom they most admired. And, despite a recording budget of just six grand and a press run of just 2,000 copies apiece, it succeeded.

Bryars continues:

> Island supported Brian's wish to have this label, which he viewed as a kind of research area for A&R, as well as being something in its own right. He had always felt that there were areas of contemporary music that need not alienate a non-specialist listener. The label also pointed to the kinds of contemporary music that he had found attractive at the time he was a student.

With Island Records' distribution, and Eno's name attached to all four of these albums as producer (and to the six that would follow in 1976 and 1978), Obscure really wasn't as obscure as it might have been. Indeed, discussing with *ZigZag* magazine a couple of years later the role of promotion and the media in his career, Eno mused, 'I would... prefer... a low-profile marketing campaign that almost said, 'Don't just buy this on trust, listen to it in case you don't like it'. The whole point of the Obscure label was to say that, actually. It was to say, 'These are records you might not like'. I think it's always better for something to be heard for what it is, rather than for reputation or anything like that'.

In fact, the label's very name aroused some hostility. Barry Miles, writing in the *New Musical Express*, bemoaned:

> Obscure Records is surely a form of inverted snobbery, certainly more designed to appeal to upmarket Sunday-supplement-reading intellectuals who want to think they're hip, than to your average rock-and-roller who has his or her ears already open for interesting new sounds. And as rock-and-rollers' ears are more open, moist, receptive and much more numerous, may I suggest Eno advertise in *New Musical Express* as well as *The Sunday Times*? There's little new or obscure on Eno's label that we haven't heard ten years ago, and the name 'Obscure' is likely to turn people off rather than introduce them to new areas. Though it is filling a need among the community of experimental musicians and composers to hear each other, Obscure is doing nothing new unless it reaches the rock audience.

Of the four albums chosen to launch the label – and that includes Eno's ambient debut *Discreet Music* – Bryars' *The Sinking of the Titanic* remains the best known and loved. Two compositions performed at the 1972 premier – the title piece and 'Jesus' Blood Never Failed Me Yet' – became sides one and two respectively of the maiden *Obscure* album, and Eno later remarked, 'I thought – still think – that those are two of the really significant pieces of music of the last 50 years, and they're both on one album. That's what I call value for money'.

By virtue of the international attention that is drawn to any event involving the sinking, raising or preservation of the doomed liner *Titanic*, that work remains Bryars' most-performed (and recorded). But 'Jesus' Blood' – a looped recording of a lone cracked voice singing the title phrase alone – is the most remarkable, and that despite what Bryars remembers as 'the occasional hiccup': 'Chris Blackwell, at Island, had a habit of having new projects playing as he spoke on the phone. When 'Jesus' Blood' was playing, he had to put the phone down, and wanted to stop the release, as he thought that the unaccompanied voice was going to be just that throughout the whole side of the LP. After all, nothing else had happened during the first three minutes or so'.

Neither was Blackwell's response the only uncertainty with which Bryars found himself needing to contend: 'I hired a number of orchestral musicians: the entire horn section, for example. None of these players wanted to be identified in the credits, as they felt it would damage their careers! By contrast, everyone on the 1993 re-recording, insisted on full credits, and this included the former concertmaster from the New York Philharmonic!'.

Bryars also contributed to *Ensemble Pieces* – five pieces recorded separately by him, the American composer John Adams (whose strident orchestrations are almost Hammer-Horror-soundtrack worthy), and Christopher Hobbs: a former member of the Scratch Orchestra. Hobbs' two contributions – the single-length 'Aran' and the longer 'McCrimmon Will Never Return' – could both, in the right light, put one in mind of some of Mike Oldfield's (later post-*Incantations*) recordings, executed, however, with a brusqueness that Oldfield would never have countenanced. Wry ears might also catch a hint of the Ivor Cutlers hanging around 'McCrimmon...'.

It was Bryars who introduced Adams to the Obscure fold: 'I'd worked in California with John in 1973 when I was guest composer at the San Francisco Conservatory of Music, where John taught'. Here, Bryars contributed '1, 2, 1-2-3-4', which he describes as 'one of a number of kind-of conceptual pieces that I did between 1969 and 1972. I was interested in what I called 'private' pieces: pieces that, in principle, only revealed partial information. This piece was written for a tour in 1971 that involved me and other composers from my circle. It drew on my memories of working at Greasborough Working Men's Club, where I was the house bass player for a year and a half. Here, each player (Andy Mackay among them) listens to music on headphones, and shadows the part for their own instrument or voice. In this way, each player hears something different (themselves and the recording), and the audience only hears what the players play, which is a kind of filtered or distilled form of the recording. It is deliberately comic'.

Eno's contribution to the catalogue – *Discreet Music* – was naturally destined to become Obscure's biggest seller, both at the time and in the years since then. (It is one of just two Obscure originals that has never fallen out of print, the other being the Penguin Cafe Orchestra's debut.) Eno claimed it cost just £3 to make, and he told *Sounds*' Vivien Goldman that 'It's my favourite record'. He pointed across the room: 'I made it sitting there, in about 35 minutes', but then admitted he was lying. 'It's the result of three different lines of experimentation, going back to '66. Like when you get the Japanese painters who grind colours all day, prepare the paper, get their seat set up and move it around, get the brushes organised and so on, and then at the end of the day, just at twilight, go 'ch ch ch', executing a rapid series of karate chops in mid-air'.

Discreet Music was, in fact, a slowed-down copy of a tape he'd recorded (under the title 'Wind On Wind') for use at the Fripp concerts back in May. To complete the album, Eno's interpretation of Johann Pachelbel's 'Canon In D Major' was worked out with Gavin Bryars, but never to Eno's satisfaction. 'Discreet Music' is an evening piece', Eno explained to *Sounds* a couple of years later. 'The other side, which I don't think is very successful, is an early-afternoon-on-a-rainy-day piece'.

Two decades on, in his *A Year With Swollen Appendices* diary, Eno observed (19 April) that Lou Reed's *Metal Machine Music* was released in the same week as *Discreet Music*. One was loud and abrasive; the other had no sound louder than tape hiss, 'and yet they occupy two ends of what was at the time a pretty new axis – music as immersion: the roots of ambient'. According to that same journal entry, he'd eaten sausages the night before.

Finally, in this initial *Obscure* batch, *New And Rediscovered Musical Instruments* introduced London Musicians Collective alumnus David Toop, with his battery of homemade 'rediscovered' instruments, and kinetic sculptor Max Eastley's 'new' ones: Heath Robinson-style devices, the musical capabilities of which often felt almost secondary to their visual complexity. Side by side, the pair contrived the most startling insertion into the Obscure catalogue – at least for listeners drawn in via their interest in Eno – an album that you could barely hear above real life's own interpretations of many of the same sounds, but which haunts with its fragile beauty.

Retailing at a penny under £2 apiece and issued just in time for Christmas (!), the Obscure series sold to the curious, and Obscure 3 kept on selling. The initial run had vanished within a fortnight; a re-pressing was gone in ten days. At the same time as Island warned Eno that his hopes of the label releasing up to eight albums a year were about twice as ambitious as they ought to be, he was also asked to ensure that the next batch included another proven – or at least potentially – best-selling composer.

Chapter Eight: We Can Guess The Rest

September 1975: Roxy Music – 'Love Is The Drug' b/w 'Sultanesque (Single)
October 1975: Roxy Music – Siren (Album)

Tracks: 'Love Is The Drug', 'End Of The Line', 'Sentimental Fool', 'Whirlwind', 'She Sells', 'Could It Happen To Me?', 'Both Ends Burning', 'Nightingale', 'Just Another High'
Produced by Chris Thomas
Recorded AIR Studios, London July - September 1975
LP Release date 24 October 1975
LP Highest chart positions: UK 4/US 50
Single Release date September 1975
Single Highest chart positions: UK: 2, US: 30

December 1975: Roxy Music – 'Both Ends Burning' b/w 'For Your Pleasure' (Live at Wembley (Single)

Personnel:
Bryan Ferry: vocals, keyboards
Andy Mackay: sax
Phil Manzanera: guitar
John Gustafson: bass
Eddie Jobson: keyboards, synthesizer
Paul Thompson: drums
The Sirenettes: backing vocals
Produced by Chris Thomas
A-side Recorded AIR Studios, London July - September 1975
B-side Wembley Empire Pool 17-18 October 1975
Release date: December 1975

Phonograph Record's Ben Edmonds was taking no prisoners. Not only did he write that Roxy Music were 'among the handful of very best bands in the world', but *Siren* was their 'most consistent album'. Maybe it lacked 'the immediate intensity of their strongest performances ('A Song For Europe', 'The Thrill Of It All'), but its 'smoothly flowing middle ground' consolidated 'the stylistic evolution of their previous four albums. And the opener 'Love Is The Drug' is danceable enough to suggest that if promotion is intelligently keyed to those Midwest markets where the band is revered, they should have their first stateside hit single'. Which they did.

When Roxy Music released 'Love Is The Drug', it was still something of a novelty for rock bands to *go disco*. Bowie, of course, had already made a move with *Young Americans* earlier in the year, and 'Fame' was still dominating the US chart as 'Love Is The Drug' took its bow. But those other artists who (or, more accurately, whose records) have since become synonymous with the conjoined genre ('Da' Ya' Think I'm Sexy?', 'I Was Made for Loving You' and so on…), were still hiding in the rocking shadows at this point, with even The Rolling Stones' *Black and Blue* album some six months off in the future. So, 'Love Is The Drug' – in reaching number 2 in the UK and 30 in America – would join 'Fame' as the most successful song of its type for another three years until The Stones' 'Miss You' blew everything out of the water.

'Love Is The Drug' is a slinky, sinewy performance built around a bass line that refuses to let you stand still and a lyric that added (though we didn't know it at the time) another weapon to Ferry's arsenal of artful mannerisms: a single line that – both in tone and intonation – is seized upon by everyone as the one that *makes the record*. Here, it's 'Lumber up, limbo down' (and later, as if to reinforce the point: 'Dim the lights/We can guess the rest'). In later years, 'Dance Away' would perfect the gesture for all time – 'You're dressed to kill/But guess who's dying' – but this is where he found the formula.

That Roxy Music embraced dance music was no surprise. Ferry's fascination with dance dated back at least as far as 'Do The Strand', even if the song itself was not obviously danceable, and his ever-growing reputation as one of the era's great socialites surely made it inevitable that he was aware of the rising disco scene, in its pre-*Saturday Night Fever* guise when subversion and perversion were the gateway drugs, and the suburban hordes had yet to batter down the doors. 'Love Is The Drug' captures that world exquisitely, and when you flipped the record over, B-side 'Sultanesque' maintained the sensation that this was actually *more* than a record: it was a manifesto (prophetic pun intended).

'Sultanesque' can be (and has been) dismissed as simply Ferry attempting to beat Eno at his own game. Taking songwriting credits on a Roxy B-side for the first time, Ferry fed his Farfisa organ through an effects box and concocted a direct-to-tape electronic drone. Eddie Jobson (who later professed to 'hate' the song) dropped by to add synthesizer, and Ferry called it good. The result was five-minutes-plus of jukebox jamming concrete that purchasers either loved to death or hated beyond reason. But it certainly prefigured what Eno would get up to when he linked with Bowie for *Low.* So it is perhaps only *just* that Bowie got his revenge in early: it was a reissue of his six-year-old 'Space Oddity' that prevented Roxy from scoring their first UK number one single.

The hit was the opening cut on the fifth Roxy Music album, released the following month. And in terms of first impressions, the artwork was as alluring as ever: Ferry's current paramour – model Jerry Hall, the future Mrs Mick Jagger and the current Mrs Rupert Murdoch – spread out on a rock off the Anglesey coast. *Rolling Stone*'s Simon Frith was not the only person to notice that 'The cover of the new Roxy Music album is credited to eight people: two more than made the music'. Frith found it effective, regardless: 'It shows a siren on the rocks, perfectly posed down to her last blue fingernail, but the lurid lighting gives the game away: it's another '50s ad. 'Come hither', she's saying, 'and buy Johnson's gin'. The song about *her* isn't the sea drama 'Whirlwind', but 'She Sells': 'Your lingerie's a gift wrap/Slip it to me'.

At some point, however, you needed to take out the record and spin the thing, and any fair-minded jury is probably *still* out on its overall merits. At the time, it was a disappointment, as though the entire record was reacting against the futuristic glow of 'Love Is The Drug', by reverting to the most straightforward type it could imagine. Indeed, even Phil Manzanera confessed that Roxy Music had somehow become 'a rock group', and that *Siren* was a rock album: 'a straight rock album'. He told the *New Musical Express*' Chris Salewicz:

I feel much more than ever before that I'm in a rock group... but still a left-of-centre rock group. Just slightly left-of-centre, which is the way I see a lot of the rock groups like The Who and Zeppelin. And all the groups that have carried on, like the Floyd... they're all slightly left or right of some centre. I think it's also like an instinct thing. It's not conscious, but it's just an instinct for survival. It's something that happens to all groups. We do head for this sort of centre-point because that's how we're going to survive. And you can do anything that's relevant to that, which I think I've sort of done with the solo projects.

Ferry too was effusive in his praise for *Siren*. He told *Disc*'s Ray Fox Cumming:

I think that it is the best album we've done. It has the energy of the first two, and the professionalism of the last two. The advantage of making a lot of albums is that you acquire the expertise to make each new one sound more and more professional. In the end, though, you get problems of knowing how much to put on each track. For *Country Life* we used a 24-track studio; this time, we used a 16-track. Everyone now is keen to play on every track, so there has to be a certain amount of discipline. There comes a time when you have to say diplomatically what you want to add on would be very nice, but it might detract from what's already there.

The problem was, with Roxy, it was often the add-ons that brought the music to life. The songs themselves are, as always, masterclasses in lyricism, but the feeling lingers that the band's eye for arrangements had been scaled back considerably and with it their sense of adventure – here the ballad ('End Of The Line'), there the off-kilter rocker ('Whirlwind'), here the grand statement ('Just Another High'), there the avant-garde interlude (the two-minute intro to 'Sentimental Fool'). Only with 'Both Ends Burning' did *Siren* truly come back to life, and even *that* glowed far brighter in concert than it ever did on vinyl – which, in turn, might explain why, when the song was released as a single, it promptly became the band's worst-performing UK 45 yet: peaking at 25 when only one of its predecessors had even missed the top 10 ('All I Want is You' reached 12). None of which is to say *Siren* is a lousy album, nor to dismiss those fans who argue that the first five Roxy Music albums represent the most coherent and consistent run of releases by any band of their era (and any other time, for that reason).

Nothing on *Siren* could be described as a betrayal of the band's earliest promise, and Bryan Ferry remained perhaps *the* key vocalist/songwriter of the glam age. But of all the musical directions that Roxy could've taken out of their debut – and which were so beautifully refined across *For Your Pleasure* – the one they had ultimately chosen to pursue, was also the line of least commercial resistance, even if their biggest hits were the ones that most-purposefully bucked that conservatism. Maybe then, it was time they took a rest? A flurry of period whispers certainly thought so, which is why the *New Musical Express*' Chris Salewicz asked Manzanera and Mackay about 'the rumours', when they talked in November 1975:

Mackay: 'Which rumours are these?'.
Salewicz: 'The one that the rock world's buzzing with: that you're both going to leave Roxy Music'.

Mackay: 'The best thing is to bet on this. There's an amazing amount of money to be made and lost'.

Manzanera: 'I'll have five-to-four on Andy Mackay to leave Roxy'.

Mackay: 'You can go for the Yankee – five bets – that all of Roxy will leave Roxy. Does it not occur to the press that there have always been split rumours? The time to worry is when there aren't any'.

Manzanera: 'My theory is that there's somebody who thinks I should leave, and if he keeps putting it in *New Musical Express* long enough, he'll convince me. I think that's absolutely true, actually'.

For now, however, the grapevine needed to find other things to mutter about as Roxy Music returned to the road in October – their first UK tour in a year, followed swiftly by their second North American visit in ten months.

02 October 1975 Guildhall, Preston
03 October 1975 Empire, Liverpool
04-05 October 1975 Leeds University, Leeds
06 October 1975 Trentham Garden, Stoke-on-Trent
08-10 October 1975 Apollo, Glasgow
12-13 October 1975 City Hall, Newcastle
14-15 October 1975 Belle Vue, Manchester
17-18 October 1975 Empire Pool, Wembley, London
22-23 October 1975 Bingley Hall, Birmingham

14 November 1975, Public Auditorium, Cleveland, OH
21 November 1975 Lisner Auditorium, Washington DC
22-23 November 1975 Massey Hall Toronto, Canada
01 December 1975 Sports Arena, Toledo, OH

23 January 1976 Konserthuset, Stockholm, Sweden
24 January 1976 Gothenburg, Sweden
27 January 1976 Konserthuset, Stockholm, Sweden

13 February 1976 Memorial Auditorium, Kansas City, MO
15 February 1976 Kent State University, Kent, OH
16 February 1976 Bowling Green State University, OH (Cancelled)
17 February 1976 Ambassador Theatre, St. Louis, MO
20-21 February 1976 Palladium, Los Angeles, CA

26 February 1976 Armadillo World Headquarters, Austin, TX
28 February 1976 Warehouse, New Orleans, LA
29 February 1976 Ellis Auditorium, Memphis, TN
06 March 1976 Orpheum Theatre, Boston, MA
07 March 1976 (unknown venue) Rochester, NY
08 March 1976 Calderone Theater, New York, NY
11 March 1976 State Fair Coliseum, Indianapolis, IN
12 March 1976 Veterans Auditorium, Columbus, OH
13 March 1976 The Gardens, Louisville, OH
14 March 1976 Carnegie Mellon University, Pittsburgh, PA
15 March 1976 Memorial Coliseum, Ft. Wayne, IN
16 March 1976 IMA Auditorium/Theater, Flint, MI
18 March 1976 Guthrie Theatre, Minneapolis, MN
20 March 1976 Defiance College Auditorium, Defiance, OH

Roxy Music's latest live show was their most exacting yet: a blindingly brilliant presentation that truly told the story so far. Shot at Wembley, the promo film for 'Both Ends Burning' caught the mood of it – the army-chic outfit; The Sirenettes (Jacqui Sullivan and Doreen Chanter) cast as the absolute epitome of impossible glamour, poised and perfect just feet behind Bryan Ferry; the rest of the band spread out around. Between that and the performance of 'Love Is The Drug' that showed up on ITV's *Supersonic* (both appear on *The Thrill of it All* - Bryan's the one wearing the eyepatch), you knew. This wasn't simply a band you wanted to like; it was one you wanted to join. And so *what* if you couldn't actually play an instrument? Neither could Eno!

Step back from the visuals: what about the music? Not only were all five albums represented, the *Siren* material immeasurably improved on its studio blueprints: check out the version of 'Both Ends Burning', which bleeps out of 'Chance Meeting' on *Viva*. Further highlights appear on the bootleg *Foolproof – The 1975 Tour Of The United States*. But better still is *Do You Think I'm A Funky Chick?* – a double album drawn from a 1976 Swedish TV broadcast preserving one of the Stockholm shows in its entirety, and proving to be a master class in both selection and pacing. (The show remains unreleased in its entirety, but five tracks appear on *The Thrill Of It All*. You can find the rest on YouTube.)

Even more exciting than the band's own repertoire was the inclusion, for the first time ever, of a handful of solo projects: Mackay's 'Wild Weekend', Manzanera's 'Diamond Head' and Ferry's 'The 'In' Crowd' and

'A Hard Rain's A-Gonna Fall'. 'It was great fun being able to play those numbers', Manzanera recalls (author interview). 'But remembering that it was a Roxy Music show, I think then things started to get a little bit out of hand, so it had to be brought back a little'.

No matter, Chris Salewicz's Wembley review in the *New Musical Express* suggested that this was the highlight of the entire show – the moment when Ferry and The Sirenettes left the stage, and the remaining quartet 'go into the title track from the guitarist's solo album *Diamond Head*':

Only now – and during the subsequent number: Mackay's ripsnorting and technically very uneven 'Wild Weekend' – does this band let on that it's been cruising in third for the last hour or so. How odd that the Roxy musical socks should only be pulled up while the maestro's away. How strange that *real* feeling only slides into the sound as Ferry slides from the stage. How pleasing that after 'Wild Weekend' the band should decide to… play with Ferry as a band member rather than as Ferry's backing band. And you know something? When Ol' Blue Hair sucks in his ego and moves back into the lineup as nothing more than a well-coutured lead vocalist, Roxy Music becomes one bitch of a rock-'n'-roll band.

December 1975: Fripp & Eno – Evening Star (Album)
Tracks: 'Wind On Water', 'Evening Star', 'Evensong', 'Wind On Wind', 'An Index Of Metals'
Personnel: Robert Fripp, Brian Eno
Produced by Brian Eno, Robert Fripp
Recorded 1974-75
Released December 1975
Highest chart positions; did not chart

A considerably *easier* listen than the duo's last excursion, *Evening Star* is often overlooked in favour of the majesty of that earlier disc. Certainly, four short tracks across side one do foretell a less-intensive immersion than before.

But 'An Index Of Metals' consuming side two is all that it should be. Taped a year or so before the album's release, the oldest recording on the album is revered by Eno biographer David Sheppard as the duo's most 'sustained tonal experiment yet'. In fact, the entire album's greatest failing is simply the fact that *(No Pussyfooting)* came first.

Compared to *(No Pussyfooting)*, there is less overt aggression in the album's tones and textures, meaning the entire experience has more in common with the ambience of later Eno solo releases. Fripp's treated-guitar contributions too look towards the unbridled Frippertronics that would be unleashed four years hence as he toured libraries, bookstores and press conferences to promote his upcoming *Exposure* album.

For now, the concept of music that you really don't need to listen to was still so alien to most potential buyers (who remained largely drawn from the Roxy, Eno and King Crimson fan bases), that Island once again put it out in their budget-priced series.

February 1976: Rock Follies – 'Sugar Mountain', b/w 'War Brides' (Single)
February 1976: Rock Follies – Rock Follies (TV series/ Soundtrack album)

Tracks: 'Sugar Mountain', 'Good Behaviour', 'Stairway', 'Daddy', 'Lamplight', 'The Road', 'Glen Miller Is Missing', 'Biba Nova', 'Talking Pictures', 'Hot Neon', 'Roller Coaster', 'Rock Follies'
CD bonus track: 'War Brides'

Spring 1976: Rock Follies – 'Glen Miller Is Missing' b/w 'Talking Pictures' (Single)

Personnel (all recordings)
Charlotte Cornwell, Julie Covington, Rula Lenska: vocals
Ray Russell: guitar
Tony Stevens: bass
Brian Chatton: keyboards
Peter Van Hooke: percussion
Robin Williams: violin
Sadie MacKenzie: backing vocals
Produced by Andy Mackay
Recorded 1975
Released February 1976
Highest chart positions: UK: 1, US: did not chart

The television series *Rock Follies* was the brainchild of writer and lyricist Howard Schuman, with music written and produced by Andy Mackay. It aired for two six-show series' on ITV during 1976 (ironically, while Mackay was out of the country, touring the United States with

Roxy Music) and 1977, and series-specific soundtrack albums perhaps inevitably accompanied it. It was originally conceived as a BBC television play called *Censored Scenes from King Kong,* before being canned and, ultimately, wholly revised. (The original play finally ran at the Open Space in London in 1977.)

It seems very tame now, but *Rock Follies* was originally considered – and perhaps designed to be – something of a shocker, tapping on each of the taboos that hamstrung British broadcasting in the mid-1970s: Bad language!; Mild alcohol and drug use!!; Vaguely sexual situations!!! And an all-female rock-'n'-roll band trying to make its way in the male-dominated world of serious (as opposed to frivolous frock-wearing pretty pop) music: *that* was the most jaw-dropping of all. Well, we say 'all-female rock-'n'-roll band', although in truth, it was only the three-strong vocal front line that was female. The musicians themselves were strictly all-male, which immediately pushed The Little Ladies (as their band was named) into a very poor third place behind the American rockers Fanny, and the cartoon combo Josie and the Pussycats when it came to living up to the show's description. Yet somehow, the show worked.

Julie Covington, Rula Lenska and Charlotte Cornwell were the ladies in question. All were considered as unknowns at the time (Covington's stint as the original Janet in *The Rocky Horror Show* was already largely forgotten), and despite the spotlight that the show placed them under, none were under any illusions of instant fame. As Covington told the *TV Times*: 'My first memories of the music business were after I made my first record and was out of work. I ended up in a store in London, actually selling my own record. Painful business, music'.

The plot lines were reasonably realistic, and Mackay's songs slid easily out of the singers' mouths, even if they did bring the rock-'n'-roll aspect of the drama into question. Writing from a direction that was wholly removed from anything we'd heard from him before, Mackay revealed himself to be extraordinarily well-versed in the sounds of the pre-rock era, to the point where The Little Ladies could easily have gone out as a Beverley Sisters tribute act had the pop biz not been kind to them.

The music critics of the age were certainly swift to condemn the show, pinpointing *Rock Follies* among the principal reasons why television should never be allowed to try and depict the truth about rock 'n 'roll – primarily because any moments that are actually worth televising would never get past the censors. But *that*, Schumann told the *New Musical*

Express, was never his plan: 'It's not intended to work on that level. It's intended to be a representation of the rock world'. And, as such, it worked.

May 1976: Bryan Ferry – Let's Stick Together' b/w 'Sea Breezes' (Single)
July 1976: Bryan Ferry – Extended Play (EP)

Tracks: 'Heart On My Sleeve', 'The Price Of Love', 'Shame, Shame, Shame', 'It's Only Love'

September 1976: Bryan Ferry – Let's Stick Together (Album)

Tracks: 'Let's Stick Together', 'Casanova', 'Sea Breezes', 'Shame, Shame, Shame', '2HB', 'The Price Of Love', 'Chance Meeting', 'It's Only Love', 'You Go To My Head', 'Re-make/Re-model', 'Heart On My Sleeve'

Personnel (all recordings):

Bryan Ferry: vocals, keyboards, harmonica

Chris Spedding: guitar

Davy O'List: guitar on 'Sea Breezes'

John Wetton: bass

Eddie Jobson: violin, synthesizer

Paul Thompson: drums

Mel Collins, Chrism Mercer: sax

Henry Lowther: trumpet

Doreen Chanter, Helen Chapelle, Martha Walker, Vicki Brown, Paddie McHugh: backing vocals

Produced by Eno

Recorded Bryan Ferry, Chris Thomas, John Punter, 1973-76

EP Release date July 1976

EP Highest chart positions: UK: 7, US: 86

LP Release date July 1976

LP Highest chart positions: UK: 19, US: 160

It's hard to say which is the most awe-inspiring element of Ferry's 'Let's Stick Together' single. The sheer passion with which he sings? The positively filthy guitar that Chris Spedding (making his debut alongside Ferry) lays down? A harmonica honking like a flight of wild geese? The middle section yelping that Jerry Hall mimed so convincingly in the video, but which certainly wasn't her in the studio? Or – speaking of the video –

the severely undernourished caterpillar that had now taken up residency across Ferry's top lip?

It was a fabulous record, though – loud and lascivious – the ideal soundtrack for that long hot summer. And Ferry kept the pressure on with the swift (by his standards) follow-up of the *Extended Play* EP of further cover versions. All would then be swept up as *Let's Stick Together* – a collector-pleasing compilation of all his non-LP singles and B-sides so far: that is, the B-sides from 'A Hard Rain's A-Gonna Fall' and 'The 'In' Crowd'; both sides of 'You Go To My Head' and 'Let's Stick Together'; the whole of *Extended Play*, and the previously-unreleased reworking of *Country Life*'s 'Casanova'.

It's an inevitably uneven selection. The singles are uniformly superb, but the Roxy covers, in particular, feel unconvincing and maybe even a shade disingenuous, almost as if Ferry – aware that he would not receive songwriting royalties from the A-sides of his hit 45s – vowed to make sure he got them from the flips, but with the least amount of effort: for which, of course, you can't really blame him. Either way, it's peculiar how Ferry discographies – and even reissue programmes (the most recent in summer 2021) – blithely sweep *Let's Stick Together* up among Ferry's regular solo albums, wholly overlooking its origins and content, leaving the impression that a man whose entire career has been devoted to fastidious thematics, one day woke up and thought 'Fuck it'. Whatever next? Plimsolls from Woolworths and a baseball cap?

Rolling Stone's Wayne Robins certainly seemed to believe that the album was the direct descendant of *These Foolish Things* and *Another Time, Another Place* – he wrote, *Let's Stick Together* is the least campy of Bryan Ferry's three solo albums. Rather than do suave interpretations of oldies as diverse as 'It's My Party' and 'A Hard Rain's A-Gonna Fall', he has chosen to blend less-loaded reworkings with reinterpretations of his own earlier work with Roxy Music ... fortify(ing) a style in which virtually all his previous songs can be recycled' – which is a neat interpretation, regardless of how wrong it might be, and one that is not without precedent either; one recalls Ferry's ambiguity on the topic of Roxy's second album simply being a re-recording of their first. Plus, few of the onboard singles and B-sides had made it to the United States; to any but the most attentive American, this probably *was* a brand new album.

Which means Ferry was taking one hell of a risk – imagine Roxy following *Country Life* with an album built around 'Sultanesque', 'Hula Kula', 'Your Application's Failed', 'The Numberer' and 'The Pride And

The Pain'?. Imagine Bowie following *Young Americans* with 'Amsterdam', 'Round And Round' and 'Velvet Goldmine'?

But Ferry got away with it, not only in the USA but in Europe, the Far East and in the UK – even the *Sunday Times* fell into the trap when Philip Norman numbered the following year's *In Your Mind* LP as 'his fourth as a solo performer'. More than the secondhand nature of the music itself, that might've been the most amazing aspect of the entire affair.

(Unreleased): Roxy Music – 'Do The Strand' (Live), 'War Brides'
July 1976: Roxy Music – Viva Roxy Music (The Live Roxy Music Album) (Album)

Personnel:

Bryan Ferry: vocals, keyboards

Andy Mackay: sax

Phil Manzanera: guitar

Rick Wills, Sal Maida, John Gustafson, John Wetton: bass

Eddie Jobson: keyboards, violin

Paul Thompson: drums

The Sirens: backing vocals

Produced by Chris Thomas

Recorded: Glasgow Apollo, 2 November 1973 (tracks 2, 4); Newcastle City Hall 27/28 October 1974 (tracks 1, 3, 6-8); Wembley Empire Pool 17/18 October 1975 (5)

Released August 1976

Highest chart positions: UK: 6, US: 81

Tracks: 'Out Of The Blue', 'Pyjamarama', 'The Bogus Man', 'Chance Meeting', 'Both Ends Burning', 'If There Is Something', 'In Every Dream Home A Heartache', 'Do The Strand'

So the rumours were true. Roxy Music had… not broken up. They were stepping back, though: taking a break, having a hiatus, whatever you want to call it. But the fans, who knew only what they read in the press, called it a split and were not reticent about making their feelings known. Ferry told *New Musical Express*' Paul Rambali:

> When (Roxy) dissolved, I got some really awful letters from kids who felt I was betraying them. They don't realise that in order for you to keep up your own interest – which is so important – you have to keep

experimenting and keep moving, trying out different things and working with different people in different places. When The Beatles broke up, I felt sad, but now I perfectly understand how any group of people who work together on a creative basis, have to move because otherwise, they'd die.

So Roxy Music *had* broken up. You don't draw an analogy with the Beatles split if you've just popped out for twenty Sobranie Cocktails. 'I was fed up with the music business', Ferry told Nick Kent three years later. 'The *Siren* tour had been dreadfully exhausting and uninspiring in terms of the band having reached a stage of incompatibility. Plus, I was getting slagged off left, right and centre, to the point where I seriously was thinking of packing it all in: just leaving the music business altogether'. This then was his farewell; Roxy's farewell; a live album recorded across the past three years of touring (hence the plethora of bass players), and flagged the previous year by the 'For Your Pleasure' B-side. The dissolution did not come as too much of a surprise. Ferry's solo ambitions were no secret, while Manzanera and Mackay, too, had proven now that they had more to offer than Roxy allowed.

Viva! draws its content from three shows – the Apollo, Glasgow in November 1973, the previously bootlegged City Hall, Newcastle gig from November 1974, and, albeit for one song only, Wembley 1975, as compiled by Phil Manzanera. It did not please everyone. Andy Mackay was particularly vocal in his unhappiness, singling out the track listing for particular scorn; it was probably no coincidence that the one co-writing credit on the album was also Manzanera's. (Although it was difficult to disagree with the choice, which was a very tasty 'Out Of The Blue'.) However, it is hard to conceive how anyone could've improved on the finished thing. The sound quality is excellent, the performances themselves ineffable, and the song selection was clearly designed as much for the longtime fan as for the casual browser; how wry that the only hit in sight should be the least successful of them all. Think how many versions of 'Virginia Plain', 'Pyjamarama' and 'Love Is The Drug' could've been squeezed onto the 20 minutes of vinyl devoured by 'In Every Dream Home A Heartache' and 'If There is Something', and then ask yourself if the band made the wrong decision.

A new single was scheduled for around the same time as the album's release, culling 'Do The Strand' from *Viva!*, backed with a Mackay composition that we'd only recently heard a few months earlier from the mouths of The Little Ladies.

Though it did make it out as one of The Little Ladies' B-sides as well, 'War Brides' had been pointedly absent from the *Rock Follies* album: presumably – we now believed – because Roxy had recorded their own version. Ultimately, the Roxy Music single was scrapped and has never been mentioned (let alone released) since. But what fun we still can have imagining Bryan Ferry announcing, 'I'll be a boogie-woogie war bride'.

Another Obscure Interlude
Late-1976: Brian Eno/Obscure Records

Obscure 5: Jan Steele/John Cage: Voices And Instruments
Tracks: 'All Day' (Steele), 'Distant Saxophones' (Steele), 'Rhapsody Spaniel' (Steele), 'Experiences No. 1' (Cage), 'Experiences No. 2' (Cage), 'The Wonderful Widow Of Eighteen Springs' (Cage), 'Forever And Sunsmell' (Cage), 'In A Landscape' (Cage)
Produced by Brian Eno

Obscure 6: Michael Nyman: Decay Music
Tracks: '1-100', 'Bell Set No. 1'
Produced by Brian Eno

Obscure 7: The Penguin Cafe Orchestra – Music From The Penguin Cafe
Tracks: 'Penguin Cafe Single', 'From The Colonies (For N.R.)', 'In A Sydney Motel', 'Surface Tension', 'Milk', 'Coronation', 'Giles Farnaby's Dream', 'Pigtail', 'The Sound Of Someone You Love Who's Going Away And It Doesn't Matter', 'Hugebaby', 'Chartered Flight
Produced by Simon Jeffes, Stephen Nye.
Executive Producer Brian Eno

Island Records' insistence that Eno offer them a headline name in the second batch of Obscure releases one year after the first, received instant gratification with the recruitment first of John Cage to the catalogue, and then by his pairing with Robert Wyatt, Fred Frith and Michael Mantler's wife, Carla Bley. Wyatt sings on two songs on Cage's side of *Voices and Instruments*: 'Experiences No. 2' and 'The Wonderful Widow Of Eighteen Strings'. Flip the disc, and American saxophonist Jan Steele contrives to make this the most accessible disc in the Obscure catalogue – and that despite being one of several that Gavin Bryars admits were released 'in spite of my opposition of them. The Cage one, for example, which I thought was very poor'.

Obscure 6 – *Decay Music* – was turned over to writer Michael Nyman, making his recorded debut with an extraordinarily-minimalist piece of work, originally written as a soundtrack to a Peter Greenaway movie that followed the progression of numbers from one to 100: an origin whose spirit it retains.

Obscure 7 introduced the world to the now-renowned Penguin Cafe Orchestra, and this gorgeous vision of multi-instrumentalist Simon Jeffes represents Obscure's second permanently-available release. Eno was credited as 'executive producer' – for the first time in the Obscure catalogue, he played no part in the recording process whatsoever.

Chapter Nine: Baying At The Moon

September 1976: 801 – 801 Live (Album)

Personnel:
Brian Eno: synth, vocals, guitar, tapes
Phil Manzanera: guitar
Bill MacCormick: bass, vocals
Lloyd Watson: slide guitar, vocals
Francis Monkman: Rhodes, clavinet
Simon Phillips: drums
Produced by 801
Recorded Queen Elizabeth Hall, London, August 1976
Released September 1976
Highest chart positions: UK: 52, US: did not chart
Tracks: 'Lagrima', 'T.N.K. (Tomorrow Never Knows)', 'East Of Asteroid', 'Rongwrong', 'Sombre Reptiles', 'Baby's On Fire', 'Diamond Head', 'Miss Shapiro', 'You Really Got Me', 'Third Uncle
Bonus Tracks: 'The Fat Lady Of Limbourg'
2009 bonus disc: (All rehearsals) 'Lagrima', 'T.N.K. (Tomorrow Never Knows)', 'East Of Asteroid', 'Rongwrong', 'Sombre Reptiles', 'The Fat Lady Of Limbourg', 'Baby's On Fire', 'Diamond Head', 'Miss Shapiro', 'You Really Got Me', 'Third Uncle', 'Lagrima (Reprise)'

Manzanera's first move following Roxy's dissolution was to convene a project which he and Eno had been discussing for some time: 801. (The name was taken from the Eno lyric 'The True Wheel'). The guitarist explains: 'What happened was, Eno left Roxy, started doing his albums, and then got persuaded by EG to go out on the road. He really didn't want to… and that was the end of his ambitions to be a conventional *pop star*. But he continued to do his recordings, and I continued to work with him, so I was around quite a lot, and at one point, we went off to a cottage somewhere and came up with this idea of doing a project which would last six weeks – putting people who loved technique and people who hated technique, together, so they could fight it out, mix it all up, and see what came out'.

Bill MacCormick was one of the first people they called. 'Phil's idea was to occupy summer '76, make some money and play some gigs in Europe in between the sessions for what became (his next non-Roxy album) *Listen Now*'. The trio of Manzanera, MacCormick and Eno, plus

Bill's brother Ian MacDonald, then decamped to a different country cottage to work out a setlist: it was MacCormick who seized upon rearranging The Beatles' 'Tomorrow Never Knows'. Bill Bruford came in on drums, Francis Monkman on keyboards. But then Bruford was out ('A large number of tracks were originally recorded with me and Bill Bruford, but it didn't quite work', explains MacCormick), at which point producer Rhett Davis (returning from the Quiet Sun/*Diamond Head* sessions) suggested Simon Phillips.

MacCormick continues: "You Really Got Me' came out of one of the rehearsals when we all suddenly found ourselves playing it. We rehearsed two other tracks off *Taking Tiger Mountain* – 'The True Wheel' and 'Mother Whale Eyeless' – I seem to recall, but they were dropped from the setlist simply because of time constraints'.

The new group's original itinerary called for them to play a string of large festivals in France, only for a riot at a similar event to provoke the French government into cancelling the rest – by which time 801 had already been in rehearsal at Island's Basing Street studios for a month. Now all eyes turned towards the Queen Elizabeth Hall show (and a warm-up gig in Cromer, Norfolk, a few nights earlier). MacCormick: 'Recording the Queen Elizabeth Hall gig was Phil's way of trying to make financial sense of the time spent', and the ensuing *801 Live* would indeed make it all worthwhile.

Vivien Goldman's review in *Sounds* set the pace for the album's reception: 'Three cheers for the Island Mobile's crystalline recording – they don't miss a lick 801 produced… and the sound's so immaculate that if it wasn't for tumultuous waves of applause phasing in and out, *Live* could pass for a studio album. The unmistakably live quality is due to the exuberance and spontaneous energy in the music; not – as in most live albums – the roughness of the sound'. If there could be any regrets, it's that 801 played only one further gig that summer: a short set at the annual Reading Festival.

Unflinchingly excellent, the repertoire combined highlights from *Mainstream*, *Diamond Head* and all three Eno albums to date, plus those show-opening-and-closing covers: 'That album got fantastic reviews all over the world', Manzanera reflects, 'and still gets mentioned; still has a very good reputation'.

Tapes of the Reading performance (28 August) do circulate in reasonable quality, and the 2009 deluxe reissue of *801 Live* included a bonus disc comprising the band's rehearsals at Shepperton Studios five days previous – a complete show in itself and an exhilarating listen as the last kinks (pun intended) are ironed out and the final changes made. We miss the bells that chime awake this version of 'Lagrima', but would we want to sacrifice the eventual opening for them? No, because there is a unique purity to the original album that the fascination of alternate versions simply cannot dent. 'If you've heard the boxed set', MacCormick adds, 'then the church bells at the end of the rehearsal CD was actually the tape we used immediately before we came on stage'.

Headphones are essential, if only for those opening passages where the sound of a railway train in one ear meets the foghorn howling in the other, and 'Lagrima' marks one of those odd moments of synchronicity in the history of rock where the two best albums of the season – this and Bowie's *Station to Station* – both employ trains and guitars to make their opening point. No wonder Eno and Bowie got on so well.

Unrecognisable from its two-minute intro, The Beatles' song 'Tomorrow Never Knows' is taken to precisely the same psychedelic conclusion which the original *Revolver* version always suggested it was heading: a point that *Rolling Stone*'s review reiterated when it raved, 'Manzanera has created one of the last – and the best – psychedelic bands in the world'.

Eno's voice is a revelation: calmer than we are maybe accustomed but effects-laden and loaded with character and quirk. Remember, the audience piling in to see 801 had absolutely no idea what to expect from the show, and one of the beauties of *801 Live* is that it not only knows that, it somehow contrives it, no matter how frequently you play it, to retain the sense of surprise that was so integral to the original performance. Indeed, the liner notes to the 2009 CD remind us that 'The band's atmospheric spaciousness and power, surprised many of the press who – reasonably enough – had been expecting something more informal and self-indulgent'.

'Rongwrong' (always the most displaced cut on the Quiet Sun album) is a majestic moment of tranquility; its segue into an awe-inspiring 'Sombre Reptiles' one of the most perfectly realised in any of the musicians' repertoires – electronic squawks and jungle percussion merging with the night; distant yelps and whispering crickets. And then, out step the lizards. David Attenborough could have shot the best video in history for this.

A soft-spoken 'Golden Hours' bleeds on vinyl into a frenetic 'Baby's On Fire', but on the CD remaster, into 'The Fat Lady Of Limbourg': a performance assumed buried until it turned up in the early-1990s on Phil Manzanera's *Collection* CD. Another compilation, the less-than-legit *Dali's Car,* also suggests 'I'll Come Running' was a part of the set – at least at Reading – but it wasn't.

Now we are into the closing stretch, as 'Baby's On Fire' blazes into a soaring 'Diamond Head', 'Miss Shapiro' shimmies and shakes with even edgier energy than her studio counterpart, and 'You Really Got Me' – underpinned by the kind of one-note keyboard that made a legend of The Stooges 'I Want To Be Your Dog' – stands out as one of the best-ever covers of the hoary old classic. And then it's encore time – a 'Third Uncle' that the audience recognises instantly, feeling faster and fatter than the LP take, but Eno doesn't miss a lyrical beat. It's the audience that is breathless at the end.

'Most live albums', the *New Musical Express* review declared, 'are of no more than token value. *801 Live* is – like Bowie's *David Live* or Dylan's *Before the Flood* – one of the exceptions that prove the rule. Who needs Roxy Music now...?'.

801 would not be repeated, at least in this form. But the band would live on.

September 1976: Eno and Harmonia '76 – Tracks & Traces (Album)

Personnel:
Brian Eno: synth, vocals, e-bass
Michael Rother: guitar, keyboards, drum machine
Dieter Moebius: synth, mini-harp
Hans-Joachim Roedelius: keyboards
Tracks: 'Vamos Companeros', 'By The Riverside', 'Luneburg Heath', 'Sometimes In Autumn', 'Weird Dream', 'Almost', 'Les Demoiselles', 'When Shade Was Born', 'Trace'
2009 bonus Tracks: 'Welcome', 'Atmosphere', 'Aubade'

It took Eno 18 months to follow up on the invitations extended to him when he accompanied Harmonia on stage in Hamburg back in 1974. But in autumn 1976, immediately following the 801 adventure, he did so, joining them at their commune headquarters in Forst, Lower Saxony, where the tracks eventually gathered as *Tracks and Traces* were recorded in an atmosphere of pure relaxation and curiosity.

Certainly, there was no intention of a commercial release at the time. Eventually issued in 1997, *Tracks & Traces* is spontaneous improvisation – four musicians simply enjoying one another's company and abilities, and all the more pleasurable for that.

Returning to London, Eno was next invited to produce the eponymous debut album by electro-punks Ultravox! – an album wrapped in the

ravaged moods and lyrical themes of collapse and decay that transported
1970s rock from the bloated pastures of the past to the futuristic dystopias
predicted by punk. Released in the new year, *Ultravox!* was unlike any
other album of the time (and certainly unlike anything else Ultravox
would ever record, with or without the exclamation point that once
was integral to their name), but few people had problems believing Eno
had produced it. Indeed, Ultravox! frontman John Foxx later admitted
there was nobody else who *could* have. Among his earliest electronic
experiments, he said, was a 'sort of loop of two tracks from *Another
Green World* – 'Becalmed' and 'Sky Saw' – played full volume'. It was his
bandmates' love of that loop which inspired them to ask Eno to produce
their first album.

Like future ventures working with Television's one-time New York
compatriots Talking Heads or delving deep into that same city's new
underground and overseeing an entire album's worth of disparate
noisemakers under the overall title of *No New York*, *Ultravox!* positioned
Eno as herald of what the UK music press would soon be terming Nu-
Musik, but which would more-comfortably declare itself as the post-punk
movement, at a time when punk itself was still establishing its frontiers.

Eno – as either a conspirator or an influence – was the magnet that
brought all the attendant disparate threads together.

Late-1976: Brian Eno – Music For Films – Director's Edition (Album)

Tracks: 'Becalmed', 'Deep Waters', 'There Is Nobody', 'Spain', ' Untitled', 'The Last
Door', 'Chemin De Fer', 'Dark Waters', 'Sparrowfall (1)', 'Sparrowfall (2)', 'Sparrowfall
(3)', 'Evening Star', 'Another Green World', 'In Dark Trees', 'Fuseli', 'Melancholy
Waltz', 'Northern Lights', 'From The Coast', 'Shell', 'Little Fishes', 'Empty Landscape',
'Reactor', 'The Secret', 'Don't Look Back', 'Marseilles', 'Final Sunset', 'Juliet'
Produced by Eno
Recorded 1975-76)
Release date 1976
Highest chart positions did not chart

Pressed in a limited edition of just 500 copies, the original 27-track *Music
for Films* drew its contents from both Eno's released and unreleased
catalogues as a promotional device behind his movie-scoring ambitions. It
succeeded. 'Final Sunset' would promptly be included in Derek Jarman's
Sebastiane (1976), and 'Slow Water' in the same director's punk-shocking

Jubilee (1977). Swiftly bootlegged, the original *Director's Edition* would be succeeded in 1978 by *Music For Films*, this time presented as 'possible soundtracks to imaginary films'. Two further volumes have appeared since then, with the full content of *Director's Edition* then appearing within Eno's *Instrumental* box set.

Meanwhile, the bulk of Eno's 1977 was devoted to two primary projects – his own fourth album and three discs with David Bowie. They were Iggy Pop's *The Idiot*, and Bowie's *Low* and *Heroes* – the second-named of which, arguably, rates among the most influential albums of the entire decade.

Late-1976: Bryan Ferry – 'She's Leaving Home' (Soundtrack recording – All This and World War II).

Personnel:

Bryan Ferry: vocals

London Symphony Orchestra

Produced by Bryan Ferry

Recorded 1976

Release date 1976

Highest chart position UK: 23, US: did not chart

Hindsight hopefully recoils at the memory, but there was a period on either side of the mid-1970s when everyone wanted to make a concept album. What The Pretty Things wrought and The Who then rendered – from The Kinks and Genesis to Fairport Convention and Bowie – the idea that a story could be set to song clung to rock's rafters by whatever batty analogy you might care to make. But within this, there lurked a conceptual sub-genre that spread the joy even wider: the all-star aggregation which hauled the superstars of the land into a spotlight which promised the world there might be a stage show!; there could be a movie!! And, if all that fails, there's always witness protection.

Oh, there were some horrors. There was the folk rock opera *The King of Elfland's Daughter*, which sadly was neither as kingly or elvish as it should've been. There was the sci-fi rock opera *Flash Fearless Versus The Zorg Women Parts 5 & 6*, which roped the likes of Alice Cooper, Jim Dandy and Maggie Bell into its hopelessly ill-conceived clutches. There was *The Butterfly Ball*: a Deep Purple spin-off which (say it softly) was actually rather good. There was the aforementioned classical jazz/prog rock opera *Peter and the Wolf*, which recruited Eno, Chris Spedding, Phil Collins, Gary Moore, Keith and Julie Tippett, Manfred Mann and

Cozy Powell into its grisly noodle soup. There was the movie version of The Beatles' *Sgt. Pepper's Lonely Hearts Club Band* – so atrocious that the co-starring Peter Frampton once complained, 'It seems every time I put a new record out, (producer Robert) Stigwood puts it out on TV somewhere: 'You want to try a new record? Hold on while we put this out. We'll destroy you again''. There was the classic novel rock opera, as Jeff Wayne adapted *The War of the Worlds* for Justin Hayward, David Essex and Richard Burton – and that one *did* make it out of the dumper, with anniversary tours, a box set full of outtakes, and even disco remixes.

And there was this – the documentary rock opera *All This and World War II*, which combined an all-covers Beatles soundtrack with footage of the war itself. Probably best remembered as Peter Gabriel's first post-Genesis project (He covered 'Strawberry Fields Forever') and the source of Rod Stewart's hit 'Get Back', it also drew the Bee Gees, Frankie Laine, Leo Sayer and Roy Wood into its clutches, and Bryan Ferry too. He offered up 'She's Leaving Home' – a lushly-orchestrated lachrymose croon which is unlikely to be included on even the most catholic best-of-Bryan compilation but was pressed into service as a B-side ('Tokyo Joe'), regardless.

February 1977: Bryan Ferry – 'This Is Tomorrow' b/w 'As The World Turns' (Single)
March 1977: Bryan Ferry – In Your Mind (Album)
Tracks: 'This Is Tomorrow', 'All Night Operator', 'One Kiss', 'Love Me Madly Again', 'Tokyo Joe', 'Party Doll', 'Rock Of Ages', 'In Your Mind'

May 1977: Bryan Ferry – 'Tokyo Joe' b/w 'She's Leaving Home' (Single)
Personnel (on all releases):
Bryan Ferry: vocals, keyboards
Chris Spedding, Neil Hubbard: guitar
John Porter, John Wetton: bass
Paul Thompson: drums
Morris Pert: percussion
Chris Mercer: sax
Martin Drover: trumpet
Ann Odell, David Skinner: keyboards
Doreen Chanter, Dyan Birch, Frank Collins, Paddy McHugh, Helen Chapelle, Jackie Sullivan: backing vocals

119

Produced by Bryan Ferry, Steve Nye
Recorded AIR Studios, 1976-77
LP Release date I February 1977
LP Highest Charting Position UK: 5, US: 126
'This is Tomorrow' release date February 1977
'This Is Tomorrow' Highest Chart Position UK 9/US did not chart
'Tokyo Joe' release date May 1977
'Tokyo Joe' Highest Chart Position UK: 15, US: did not chart

One single, an EP and a compilation album notwithstanding, it was 18 months since Bryan Ferry was last heard of: a lifetime in pop terms in the 1970s. Add to that the utter redistribution of musical credibility engendered by the newborn punk rockers – and to that, the plaudits that greeted Eno's just-released work with Bowie – and it was clear that Ferry needed to draw something especially magical out of the hat this time around.

He succeeded. At first. 'This Is Tomorrow' drifts in slowly, a chorus of crickets around his smoothest croon, all about the hush of evening and a night in June, the ghost of a chorus, and then, kerpow! The band kicks in – Chris Spedding littering spare guitar lines around the rocket-propulsion rhythm; Ferry upping his vocal game accordingly as the whole thing lurches into a rockabilly shimmy, and more, still more. Spedding drops an electrifying solo without breaking a sweat, the video is street-cool personified (Bryan even wears shades for the occasion!), the band blazes on, and the end is so unexpected, your surprise can only echo its dying fade: 'Oooo...'.

The flip is less revelatory but equally exquisite – one of Ferry's most nakedly-beautiful love songs, orchestrated by Eddie Jobson and interrupted by Robert Fripp. The only question is, how did it evade inclusion on the parent album, particularly given the quality of the songs that could've made way for it?

For the first time (bass players notwithstanding), Ferry worked with minimal Roxy involvement – Paul Thompson alone attended the sessions; in his old bandmates' stead, Ferry drew from across the session-musician spectrum, a mix of recently-familiar faces (Chris Spedding, David Skinner, Chris Mercer) and strangers. The heart of early-1970s hitmakers Arrival were among the backing vocalists. The result was an album that was certainly very well-performed and produced. But it was also one that eschewed any point of comparison with Roxy Music, and felt strangely lifeless accordingly. 'All Night Operator' and 'Party Doll' aren't even Ferry-by-numbers, while repeated listens to the album's second single 'Tokyo Joe' (originally penned, apparently, as a salute to Ferry's growing Japanese following) find it swiftly transforming from tribute to parody.

More than once, as *In Your Mind* played on, one wondered whether Ferry was even aware of what was going on in the studio. Was he purposefully hamstringing the handful of songs that truly merited attention ('One Kiss', 'Rock Of Ages', the title track)? Or was it simply bad luck that left the listener wondering, what would Andy Mackay have done there?; what would Phil Manzanera have played instead? And what would the old band have made of 'Love Me Madly Again'? Such comparisons are, of course, grossly unjust. If Ferry had wanted to make a Roxy Music album, he would have – even irrevocable splits can be repaired, and Roxy's was nowhere close to *that* permanent.

The feeling that Ferry was feeling somewhat adrift, however, is unavoidable. After all, *In Your Mind* was the first time he had ever entered the studio with a full album's worth of self-composed songs and no full-time band members to help knock them into shape. What was especially confounding was, in concert, Ferry was putting on some of the best shows of his life – and *that*, despite undertaking the most extensive bout of touring of his entire career (albeit after being forced to cancel and reschedule the original 17 UK dates through December 1976).

01 February 1977 Gaumont, Southampton
02 February 1977 Winter Gardens, Bournemouth
03 February 1977 De Montford Hall, Leicester
04 February 1977 ABC, Peterborough
07-09 February 1977 Royal Albert Hall, London
12 February 1977 Capitol Theatre, Cardiff, Wales
13 February 1977 Colston Hall, Bristol
15-16 February 1977 Odeon, Birmingham
17 February 1977 Opera House, Manchester
19 February 1977 Grand Theatre, Leeds
20-21 February 1977 City Hall, Newcastle
23-24 February 1977 Apollo, Glasgow
25 February 1977 Playhouse, Edinburgh
27 February 1977 Empire, Liverpool
28 February 1977 City Hall, Sheffield
02 March 1977 Jaap Edenhal, Amsterdam, Holland

04 March 1977 Pavillon de Paris, Porte de Pantin, France
07 March 1977 Philipshalle, Düsseldorf, Germany
10 March 1977 Konserhuset, Stockholm, Sweden
12th March 1977 Scandinavium, Göteborg, Sweden
14th March 1977 Tivoli Concert Hall, Copenhagen, Denmark

12-13 May 1977 Festival Hall, Brisbane, Australia
15-17 May 1977 Hordern Pavilion, Sydney, Australia
19-20 May 1977 Festival Hall, Melbourne, Australia
25-26 May 1977 Apollo Stadium, Adelaide, Australia
30-31 May 1977 Entertainment Centre, Perth, Australia

04 June 1977 Festival Hall, Osaka, Japan
05 June 1977 Shinjuku Kouseinenkin-Kaikan, Tokyo, Japan
06 June 1977 Kouseinenkin-Kaikan, Osaka, Japan
09 June 1977 Sun Plaza, Nakano, Japan

11 June 1977 Winterland, San Francisco, CA
12 June 1977 Civic Auditorium, Santa Monica, CA
13 June 1977 University Of The Pacific, Stockton, CA
15 June 1977 Paramount Theater, Seattle, WA
19 June 1977 Tower Theater, Philadelphia PA
22 June 1977 Lisner Auditorium, Washington DC
23-24 June 1977 Bottom Line, New York
25 June 1977 Cape Cod Civic Center, South Yarmouth, MA
27 June 1977 Music Hall, Cleveland, OH
28 June 1977 Masonic Auditorium, Detroit MI

15 July 1977 Hodern Pavillion, Sydney, Australia
19 July 1977 Hodern Pavillion, Sydney, Australia
25-27 July 1977 State Theatre, Sydney, Australia

History insists that Ferry's reinvention of himself as a post-Roxy garage rocker was not among his most successful moves. But it was definitely one of his most exciting. The original Roxy, after all, were a primal influence on the young punks running around the UK in 1976/1977, and now the boot was on the other foot. With Chris Spedding (a Sex Pistols production credit under his belt) on guitar and a repertoire that breathed dirty 1960s garage fire, Ferry donned the leather trousers and went out with a show which could not have been further from the tuxedos and chic of old.

The result was a show that recast Roxy oldies and realigned the new album's mouldies – 'All Night Operator' was suddenly a Stax classic, 'In Your Mind' was more stately-grand than ever before, and 'This is Tomorrow' was seething-sleaze par excellence. A newly worked-up 'Roadrunner' joined 'Lets Stick Together', 'Shame, Shame Shame' and 'The 'In' Crowd' among the scene-setting oldies. The only existing recordings from this era are, sadly, less than the highest of fi. Nevertheless, bootlegs from Amsterdam and Gothenburg on the European leg, Tokyo and one of the July nights in Sydney, and the Bottom Line, New York, are the aural equivalents of the greatest energy drink on earth.

The opening act for the UK gigs was Island labelmates Illusion: the partial reunion of the original Renaissance, featuring Jim McCarty and Jane Relf. McCarty recalls, 'He had a very good band, with a group of backing singers that were pretty special. We didn't socialise too much, shy as we were, but Bryan always seemed nice'.

May 1977: Rock Follies – 'OK?'/'B-Side' (Single – A-side performance credited to Julie Covington, Charlotte Conrnwell, Rula Lenska, Sue Jones Davis; B-side to Charlotte Cornwell)
May 1977: Rock Follies – Rock Follies of 77 (Album)

Personnel:
Charlotte Cornwell, Julie Covington, Rula Lenska, Sue Jones-Davies: vocals
Ray Russell: guitar
Tony Stevens: bass
Peter Van Hooke: drums
Chris Parren: keyboards
Gavin Wright: violin
Andy Mackay: sax
Produced by Andy Mackay
Recorded AIR Studios, London 1977
Released May 1977
Highest chart positions: UK: 13, US: did not chart
Tracks: 'Follies Of '77', 'Struttin' Ground', 'Round 1', 'The Hype', 'Dee's Hype', 'The Things You Have To Do', 'The Band Who Wouldn't Die', 'Wolf At The Door', 'Loose Change', 'Jubilee', 'OK?', 'Real Life'
CD bonus track: 'B-Side'

Following on from the commercial (if not critical) success of the original

*Rock Follie*s series, the Little Ladies were back for a second series and a second soundtrack album too. It was a harder-hitting outing all around. Success had bred new confidence among writers and cast alike, while guest appearances from Covington's old *Rocky Horror* mates Tim Curry and Little Nell brought their peculiar dynamics into play as well. Musically too, *Rock Follies of 77* was grittier, sassier – 'You want to do me', announces the first single 'OK?', 'But I don't want to be done'. 'The Band Who Wouldn't Die' was an entertaining pub-rock highlight, while 'Jubilee' – ostensibly a celebration of the Queen's upcoming Silver Jubilee extravaganza – was a true skunk in Dior's clothing. It kicks off, and you're quavering before a squeaky-clean evocation of how the whole world needed to visit Britain for the occasion. And then the mood swings on a sixpence, and here comes the bitter warning – 'But keep well away from my street/10% are out of work', and then a pause… 'Sorry, 12% are out of work'.

June 1977: Eno and Cluster – Cluster & Eno (Album)
Personnel:
Hans-Joachim Roedelius, Dieter Moebius, Brian Eno, Holger Czukay: bass
Okko Bekker: guitar
Asmus Tietchens: synth
Tracks: 'Ho Renomo', 'Schöne Hände', 'Steinsame', 'Wehrmut', 'Mit Simaen', 'Selange', 'Die Bunge', 'One', 'Für Luise'
Produced by Connie Plank, Cluster
Recorded Conny's Studio, Cologne, June 1977
Released 1977
Highest chart positions: did not chart

A key document in the ongoing development of ambient music, say its admirers; a fairly boring sequence of loops, drones and ghostly melodies, reply its detractors. And it must be said that *Cluster & Eno*'s subsequent fame owes more to the nature of its creators than to anything they actually achieved during those few weeks spent in producer Conny Plank's studio. That said, *Cluster & Eno* is a spellbinding album – melody and texture woven together seamlessly – even if the ideas on display definitely deserve far longer running times than they are granted on the album itself. At a shade over five minutes apiece, the opening and closing cuts 'Ho Renomo' and 'Für Luise' are the album's longest, but how much more impressive 'Mit Simaen' might've been had it been expanded beyond 93 seconds.

An even-less-relaxed vision of the partnership would in fact, be delivered by a second album from the same partnership: the near-rock flavoured *After The Heat*, for which Moebius and Roedelius dropped the Cluster identity and collaborated under their surnames instead. The insistently metronomic 'Selange' from the earlier album points the direction that this second set would follow.

It is ironic then that perhaps the best indication of the partnership's promise is also the least listenable of them all: a hiss-heavy audience recording of a concert they gave in Paris on 1 November. All sustained notes and growling sonics, the music makes few concessions and takes even fewer prisoners.

Chapter Ten: The Stars Were Meant For You

September 1977: Phil Manzanera/801 – Flight 19' b/w 'Car Rhumba' (Single)
September 1977: Phil Manzanera/801 – Listen Now (Album)

Personnel:

Simon Ainley: vocals

Phil Manzanera: guitar

Bill MacCormick: bass, vocals

Brian Eno: synthesizer

Bill Livsey, Eddie Jobson, Eddie Rayner: piano

Rhett Davies: organ

Francis Monkman: piano, synthesizer

Dave Mattacks: drums

Simon Phillips: drums, percussion

Paul Thompson: drums on CD bonus tracks

Kevin Godley: vocals, percussion

Lol Creme: gizmo

Ian MacCormick: harmonica

Tim Finn, Alan Lee: backing vocals

John White: tuba

Mel Collins: sax

Produced by Phil Manzanera

Recorded Basing Street Studios 1975-1977

Released September 1977

Highest chart positiions: did not chart

Tracks: 'Listen Now', 'Flight 19', 'Island', 'Law And Order', 'Que?', 'City Of Light', 'Initial Speed', 'Postcard Love', 'That Falling Feeling'

Bonus tracks on 2000 CD: 'Blue Grey Uniform', 'Remote Control'

Additional bonus tracks on 2019 CD: 'Remote Control', 'Listen Now' (Velvet Season and the Hearts of Gold remix), 'Island' (Secret Fingers remix)

After the sheer glory that was *801 Live,* any attempt to bottle again the magic that was conjured the first time around, was doomed to… not failure, but certainly a lot more inspection and expectation than it might ordinarily have merited. Thus the band was on a hiding to nothing as *Listen Now* came together. Even with unheard elements from the earlier sessions on display, the loss of Eno's vocals was a pronounced disadvantage. Gone too was the adorable quirk that his compositions brought – far more sporting for all concerned would've been to ally *Listen Now* with *Diamond Head*, in which case it made a terrific follow-up.

Jon Savage in *Sounds* summed up many listeners' dislocation by admitting that he was dislocated himself. *801 Live*, he said, inspired him because it 'seemed an album of joyous risks, like the riotous punning of 'Miss Shapiro''. *Listen Now,* however, 'is more calculating, consistent and cold-blooded. Objectively, this album is too excellent not to be rewarded star-wise. But personally, a lack of vitality – a certain coldness at the centre – worries me. What they want, I don't know: money?; cultural subversion? But some parts I really do like'.

The funky bass line that drives 'Listen Now' is certainly a close cousin of 'Love Is The Drug', even if it does intend heading in a wholly different direction; 'Flight 19' has a gorgeous 1950s death-song feel to it, and is bisected by a wonderfully characteristic Manzanera solo; 'Island' is soft and contemplative, and 'Que?' is quick and quirky. And any sense that a few of the songs are a little samey, is mitigated by the lineup shifting from song to song.

Manzanera and MacCormick were the lone constant factor across the entire album, with drums split between Simon Phillips and Fairport Convention's Dave Mattacks (and, on one occasion, vocalist Simon Ainley), while guests simply came and went. Paramount among these was Kevin Godley, whose distinctive vocals are first heard during 'Listen Now', before he takes near-centre stage for 'Flight 19'. Even more impressively, he's joined by regular partner Lol Creme across 'Initial Speed' – a number that is absolutely glorified by the presence of their gizmo: a guitar attachment they invented and which they were in the process of launching onto the market: 'We met Phil through (PR agent) Lynn Franks when we moved down south', recalls Godley, 'although we didn't actually work with him until after Roxy'. Manzanera went on to co-produce and co-write a couple of tracks on the duo's *Freeze Frame* album in 1979, while Godley & Creme also guested on 801's 1977 tour: the duo's first live appearances since headlining Knebworth with their old band 10cc.

2 November 1977: 801 – Live at Manchester University (Album)

Personnel:
Simon Ainley: vocals
Phil Manzanera: guitar

Bill MacCormick: bass
Dave Skinner: keyboards
Paul Thompson: drums
Kevin Godley: vocals
Lol Creme: backing vocals
Produced by uncredited
Recorded Manchester University, 2 November 1977
Tracks: 'TNK', 'Flight 19', 'Listen Now', 'Law And Order', 'Diamond Head', 'Out Of The Blue', 'Remote Control', 'Miss Shapiro', 'You Really Got Me'

22 November 1977: Phil Manzanera and 801 – John Peel Show
Personnel:
Simon Ainley: vocals
Phil Manzanera: guitar
Bill MacCormick: bass
Dave Skinner: keyboards
Paul Thompson: drums
Produced by Tony Wilson
Recorded Maida Vale 4, 14 November 1977
Tracks: 'Remote Control'*, 'Law And Order'*, 'Falling Feeling'*, 'Out Of The Blue'
*Available on The Manzanera Archives Rare One

Released by Manzanera's Expression Records in 2001, this excellent recording of 801's Manchester show does not quite live up to the standards of 801's last live album, but what could? It reveals, however, what a tight outfit the band had become, and that despite what the *New Musical Express*' Paul Rambali (reviewing the earlier Victoria Palace show) described as 'the stiffness with which they played it and the confusion of styles. In spite of all this, I actually like most of the music 801 played. Manzanera and Simon Ainley's guitars, lock in shrill interplay, Paul Thompson's drums pin down hard, and Lol Creme and Kevin Godley stand at the back, adding distinctive backing vocals, sheet music and beer'.

The same lineup – less Godley & Creme – convened again for a Peel session that substantially improves upon the *Listen Now* album versions – the rearranged 'Law And Order' so beautifully adorned by Skinner's keyboards, is an especial treat; 'Remote Control' seethes anew, and 'That Falling Feeling' positively shimmers. Five years before, Bryan Ferry had mused on the possibility of Roxy Music recording their second album to the same restrictions as their own John Peel sessions. On this evidence, one wishes 801 had followed a similar whim.

November 1977: Roxy Music – 'Virginia Plain', 'Pyjamarama' (Single)
November 1977: Roxy Music Greatest Hits (Album)

Personnel: See original releases

Tracks: 'Virginia Plain', 'Do The Strand', 'All I Want Is You', 'Out Of The Blue', 'Pyjamarama', 'Editions Of You', 'Love Is The Drug', 'Mother Of Pearl', 'A Song For Europe', 'The Thrill Of It All', 'Street Life'

Were Roxy already scheming a return, allowing this to be released to test the water? If so, the portents could only be regarded as encouraging. The single rose to number 11, the album to 20, and the music papers seemed suddenly to be hosting a veritable procession of punk stars willing to discuss their own teenaged love for Roxy Music: 'Our influences were the Roxy Musics, David Bowies, T. Rexs, a twisted sexuality, a black humour which was different', recalled Siouxsie and the Banshees' Steve Severin, before reminiscing about getting dressed up for Roxy's 1975 Empire Pool performance. And he was not alone.

The band's music was leeching into the punk/new wave repertoire, either directly (Spizz Energi's cover of 'Virginia Plain') or otherwise (Simple Minds' aforementioned hijack for 'Chelsea Girl'). Both Rikki and the Last Days of Earth, and Japan, rode into view on vocals that many a critic would compare to Bryan Ferry's. And, off in his own world but a part of ours regardless, Eno's continued questing was adding further muscle to the Roxy revival, first through his role in the rejuvenation of David Bowie (Low and Heroes) and Iggy Pop (*The Idiot*, all three released during 1977), then with his own next album.

December 1977: Eno – Before and After Science (Album)

Personnel:

Brian Eno: guitar, piano, synth, vocals

Percy Jones, Paul Rudolph, Bill MacCormick, Brian Turrington: bass

Phil Collins, Andy Fraser: drums

Rhett Davies: gong

Jaki Liebezeit, Dave Mattacks: drums

Shirley Williams (aka Robert Wyatt): timbales
Kurt Schwitters: vocals
Fred Frith, Phil Manzanera: guitar
Achim (aka Hans Joachim) Roedelius, Mobi (aka Dieter) Moebius: keyboards
Snatch: vocals on 'R.A.F.'
Produced by Eno
Recorded Basing Street Studios, London; Connie Plank's studio, Cologne, 1977
Release date December 1977
Highest chart positions did not chart
Tracks: 'No One Receiving', 'Backwater', 'Kurt's Rejoinder', 'Energy Fools The Magician', 'King's Lead Hat', 'Here He Comes', 'Julie With ...', 'By This River', 'Through Hollow Lands'
(For Harold Budd), 'Spider And I'

January 1978: Eno – 'King's Lead Hat' b/w 'R.A.F.' (Single)
(Personnel see above)

When music historians reflect back on Eno's full career, and file his albums into the most convenient slots, *Before and After Science* is where the first of the ensuing categories closes. It was – until the early-1990s brought renewed interest in the field – the last of his overtly song-driven albums; his last rock record; the final link in the chain woven by *Here Come The Warm Jets*, *Taking Tiger Mountain* and *Another Green World*.

In truth, much had already changed. Perhaps it dates back to that ill-fated union with Television, and the realisation that even within a rock framework, there was room for his musical ideas without him actually having to execute them himself. But suddenly, alienation and dislocation were Eno's accepted musical default settings; of course, those were among the principles he brought to the Bowie albums, but even his contribution to Camel's *Rain Dance* album in 1977 – spooky Minimoog and piano on 'Elke' – seemed somehow foreboding. *Before and After Science* was the album that this same flurry of activity drew from Eno – a short sharp set that was distinctly informed by the spikiness of punk, as it morphed into what would later be marketed as the new wave – released the following year. And it was the scratchiest one of them all.

Recorded with a firm but constantly shifting coterie of musicians (Several tracks were recorded by Eno and a chosen bassist alone), the album glides through all the expected textures, but rarely repeats itself.

Familiarity is not at risk, and slices of pure ambience rattle with sharp pop – 'Here He Comes' could've dignified *Another Green World*; 'Energy Fools The Magician' would've clung comfortably to *Music For Films*. And while 'King's Lead Hat' (its title an anagram of Talking Heads) and 'R.A.F.' recorded with Judy Nylon's own New York no wave band Snatch made a ferocious single in the new year, across the album, they scarcely even stood out – and that despite the very audible presence of both Manzanera and Fripp behind the word games.

It was the overall construction of *Before and After Science* that rendered it so wholly different to any album that Eno had recorded in the past; a signpost to his own future, without offering more than the vaguest notion of what that future might hold. But it would be nothing like the past.

May 1978: Bryan Ferry – 'What Goes On' b/w 'Casanova' (Single)
July 1978: Bryan Ferry – 'Sign Of The Times' b/w 'Four Letter Love' (Single)
October 1978: Bryan Ferry – 'Carrickfergus' b/w 'When She Walks In The Room' (Single)
September 1978: Bryan Ferry – The Bride Stripped Bare (Album)

Personnel:

Bryan Ferry: vocals, keyboards

Waddy Wachtel, Neil Hubbard: guitar

Alan Spenner, John Wetton, Herbie Flowers: bass

Ann Odell: keyboards

Steve Nye: piano

Rick Marotta, Preston Heyman: drums

Mel Collins: sax

Martin Drover: trumpet

Produced by Bryan Ferry, Steve Nye, Simon Puxley, Waddy Wachtel, Rick Marotta

Recorded Mountain Studios, Montreux, Atlantic Studios, 1977

Release date 1 September 1978

Highest chart positions: UK 13/US 159

'What Goes On' Release date 1 September 1978

'What Goes On' Highest chart positions: UK 67/US did not chart

'Sign Of The Times' Release date 1 September 1978

'Sign Of The Times' Highest chart positions: UK 37/US did not chart

'Carrickfergus' Release date 1 September 1978

'Carrickfergus' Highest chart positions: did not chart
Tracks: 'Sign Of The Times', 'Can't Let Go', 'Hold On (I'm Coming)', 'The Same Old
Blues', 'When She Walks In The Room', 'Take Me To The River', 'What Goes On',
'Carrickfergus', 'That's How Strong My Love Is', 'This Island Earth'

It's unlikely many people rank *The Bride Stripped Bare* among Bryan
Ferry's finest releases. *Sounds'* Vivien Goldman went so far as to claim,
'Frankly, I wouldn't recommend my worst enemy to buy this album. When
the highest praise you can lavish is to recommend the artist's choice of
material – and that's just about it – you'd be better off spending a fiver at
a Safari Park, for lasting entertainment value'.

Ferry's label, too, were unhappy. They had pushed for Ferry to record
his next album in the US, with crack American session men and a top
American producer. But, he told the *New Musical Express*: 'I resisted all
of the pressures to do that: which came from several directions. I don't
want to appear smug, I just worked very hard for three months under very
strange circumstances'.

He did make a couple of concessions – guitarist Waddy Wachtel was
borrowed from Linda Ronstadt's band; drummer Rick Marotta had spent
the last five years playing with everyone from James Taylor to Steely Dan,
Phoebe Snow to Dean Friedman, and yes, Ronstadt as well. But still Ferry
stuck to his guns, and the end result was… an album that a lot of people
didn't like – which is a shame because if it's doom-and-gloom that you're
searching for (alongside the aforementioned peerless choice of material),
it's one of Ferry's most coherent concepts yet.

Bereft, it seems, following the breakup of his two-year relationship with
model Jerry Hall, Ferry threw himself into a period of such introspection
that even his pen dried up. There are just four new Ferry songs in sight,
beginning with the brief, bitter, but so ineffably-propulsive 'Sign Of The
Times' – its video Kraftwerk-styled around Bryan's newly-found beard. In
years to come, Robert Palmer would build his entire MTV career around
the rudiments of this video.

The insistent (and excellent) 'Can't Let Go', 'This Island Earth' (opening
line, 'I send myself an SOS') and the self-explanatory 'When She Walks In
The Room', were his other compositions, but only the latter was written
after Hall's departure, and one listen tells you that's true. As Nick Kent
wrote for the New Musical Express, that song is 'an unembellished *cri
de coeur* that further helped *Bride* to become easily Ferry's finest solo
effort. Indeed, it is a ridiculously underrated effort, and in time will be

regarded as a key work in the completed works of Bryan Ferry, for here is a true *soul* album… and an anguished exploration into the realism of star-crossed experience, with not a whiff of that long-patented camp that so often seemed Ferry's compositional trump. Devoid of posing, a gruelling sense of anguish lurks just beneath the surface sheen of the superb session musicianship.

For the bulk of the record, Ferry does what we all do when we get dumped (especially if we're dumped for Mick Jagger): he went back to the records that sustained him in the past; old favourites that seem to say something comforting; cuddly toys for cool adolescents – 1960s Stax chest-beaters 'Hold On (I'm Coming)' (Sam and Dave) and 'That's How Strong My Love Is' (Otis Redding: one of Ferry's lifelong idols); J. J. Cale's 'Same Old Blues'; Al Green's 'Take Me To The River'; the Velvet Underground's 'What Goes On', and most surprisingly of all, a positively-shimmering version of the 19th-century Irish folk lament 'Carrickfergus'. Of them all, it's the Green and Velvet Underground numbers that raised the highest eyebrows among the most watchful observers – the latter was a staple of Eno's admittedly-brief first solo tour; the former had recently been revived by America's Talking Heads for whom it was produced by… Eno.

It's probably coincidence, but there must've been a modicum of satisfaction for Ferry to glean, as his 'River' flows so much more enjoyably than the New Yorkers' startled-insect dissection. His 'What Goes On' on the other hand, could've been left on the cutting room floor, along with a video that does what would once have seemed impossible: it makes Ferry look awkward and retreats into the realms of trick photography to try and compensate.

Perhaps the biggest change evinced by the covers was in Ferry's delivery – a point that *Melody Maker*'s Penny Valentine hit square on the head: 'Ferry makes a passable job of turning into something of a *straight* rock singer: an interesting departure. When he used to sing 'It's My Party And I'll Cry If I Want To', you knew he didn't really mean it. Now you're not so sure'.

Across such a heartfelt and, yes, coherent album, it feels almost disrespectful that anything so crass as a *hit single* should've been sought. But Polydor (the new owners of the EG Management company's catalogue) had no such scruples – no less than three 45s were pulled from *The Bride Stripped Bare*, and it's almost gratifying to note that not *one* did well: 'What Goes On' crashed at number 67 despite an appearance on

Top of the Pops, 'Sign Of The Times' foundered at 37, and 'Carrickfergus' might as well have not existed: so little attention did it garner.

The album, on the other hand, got to number 13, which was at least respectable.

October 1978: Manzanera – 'Remote Control' b/w 'K-Scope' (Single)
October 1978: Manzanera – K-Scope (Album)
Personnel:
Tim Finn: vocals
Phil Manzanera: guitar, keyboards, synthesizer
Simon Ainley: rhythm guitar
Bill MacCormick, John Wetton: bass, vocals
Dave Skinner, Eddie Rayner: piano
Francis Monkman: piano, synthesizer
Simon Phillips: drums, percussion
Paul Thompson: drums on 'Remote Control', 'Slow Motion TV'
Kevin Godley, Neil Finn: backing vocals
Lol Creme: gizmo
Mel Collins: sax
Produced by Phil Manzanera
Recorded Sun Park Studios, Surrey, March-May 1978
Released October 1978
Highest chart positions: did not chart
Tracks: 'K-Scope', 'Remote Control', 'Cuban Crisis', 'Hot Spot', 'Numbers', 'Slow Motion TV', 'Gone Flying', 'N-Shift', 'Walking Through Heaven's Door', 'You Are Here'
CD bonus tracks: 'Remote Control' (Live 1977), 'Out Of The Blue' (Live 1977), 'It Don't Matter To Me' (Demo)

Credited to the suddenly singularly-named Manzanera, *K-Scope* is very much the son of *Listen Now* – familiar players, similar sounds, returning guests, and, it turned out, at least partly recorded during the earlier album's sessions. But it is also a reaction to its predecessor, as Manzanera explained to *Trouser Press*:

> When I finished *Listen Now*, I suddenly realized that the whole message idea had gone a bit too far over the top, and it got very depressing. I wanted to go on to a new album, so I decided to write K-Scope with Bill and Ian MacCormick instead of with the guys from 801. So we just spent

a month writing, and then we recorded it in six weeks at Chris Squire's studio.

Objectively, it must be conceded that there remains a vague sensation of *deja vu* throughout, although the addition of Neil Finn to the lead vocal booth does bring a sense of Split Enz to the proceedings (Manzanera produced several of the New Zealand outfit's albums). At the same time, however, the music is clearly moving more towards new wave immediacy than the lingering proggy, jazz overtones that hung over *Listen Now*, with the single 'Remote Control' an especially propulsive beast. Having said that, the very next track – 'Cuban Crisis' – is powered by a bass line that Quiet Sun would've adored. And talking of bass lines, John Wetton turns in a sterling performance – as both bassist and vocalist – on the moody 'Numbers'.

On this occasion, however, the album's very eclecticism could be (and was) held against it. Reviewing *K-Scope* for *Trouser Press*, Jon Young observed:

Of course, it sounds just great. That's to be expected when the likes of Simon Phillips, Mel Collins and Bill MacCormick get together with the moody guitar hero. Whether it goes anywhere, is another matter. The one thing noticeably missing is a sense of dynamics: in the playing, in the writing, and in the arrangements. On each of three instrumentals, Phil and band hit a groove and doggedly hold it, seemingly unaware of the idea of a non-vocal number as a song with a beginning, middle and end. The vocal tunes suffer from the same distant efficiency.

Godley & Creme, too, returned – the latest step in what turned out to be a lasting partnership. Godley would still be guesting on Manzanera's albums into the mid-1980s. The trio also conceived their own recording studio: Gallery Studios, in Cheam. Manzanera recalls:

They had a history of working in control rooms, using desks as an instrument. I continued with that idea, although we didn't build the studio together; in the end, they had to pull out for financial reasons. But I continued, and ended up with the biggest control room in Europe at that time, designed for bands to create and play in the control room.

The compilation *The Manzanera Archives Rare One* includes one outtake from the *K-Scope* sessions: Simon Ainley's 'Down'.

October 1978: Andy Mackay – 'A Song Of Friendship' b/w 'Skill And Sweat' (Single)
October 1978: Andy Mackay – Resolving Contradictions (Album)

Personnel:

Andy Mackay: sax, oboe, cor anglais, tin whistle, flageolet, piano, synthesizer

Ray Russell: guitar

Tony Stevens, Mo Foster: bass

Chris Parren: keyboards

Paul Thompson, Peter Van Hooke: drums

Tim Wheater: flute

Gavin Wright: violin

Michael Laird: trumpet

Produced by Andy Mackay

Recorded Basing Street Studios, March-July 1978

Released October 1978

Highest chart positions: did not chart

Tracks: 'Iron Blossom', 'Trumpets On The Mountains', 'Off To Work', 'Unreal City', 'The Loyang Tractor Factory', 'Rivers', 'Battersea Rise', 'Skill And Sweat', 'The Ortolan Bunting (A Sparrow's Fall)', 'The Inexorable Sequence', 'A Song For Friendship (The Renmin Hotel)', 'Alloy Blossom (Trumpets In The Suburbs)', 'Green And Gold'

Largely recorded with the same crew he convened for the *Rock Follies* sessions, Andy Mackay's second solo outing is a very different creature to his debut. Composed – we were told – around Mackay's long-standing interest in China, it was neither bad nor boring; it was simply underwhelming – a few steps up from easy listening; a sideways hop away from television soundtrack work. And being as that was consuming much of Mackay's time in the late-1970s, there's no surprise there. He was responsible for the theme music to the popular drama series *Armchair Theatre* and for the so-fondly-remembered detective thriller *Hazell*; indeed, his 'Theme From 'Hazell'' became the first-ever hit for former Stone The Crows singer Maggie Bell in 1978. 'Lots of people have said to me I've done better things', Bell admitted to *Melody Maker*, 'but when I first listened to the backing track of 'Hazell', it reminded me of early John Mayall stuff. It's a 12-bar blues. How commercial can you get with a 12-bar blues?'.

Mackay also returned to session work. John Cale recruited him to play on an early Squeeze session. In addition, he guested on releases by Pavlov's Dog, Eddie and the Hot Rods, Mickey Jupp, Johnny Cougar, Godley & Creme, and *Rock Follies* guitarist Ray Russell's version of 'The Clapping Song'. Amidst so much activity, one wonders quite what *Resolving Contradictions* was meant to achieve, beyond making Roxy Music fans wonder just how ironically Mackay intended its title to be – for, within just a few months, he and his bandmates would indeed have resolved any contradictions they may have felt: Roxy Music was back together, and they still denied they had ever really been away.

The Final Obscure Interlude
Late-1978: Brian Eno/Obscure Records
Obscure 8: John White/Gavin Bryars – Machine Music
Tracks: 'Autumn Countdown Machine', 'Sons Of Gothic Chord', 'Jew's Harp Machine', 'Drinking And Hooting Machine', 'The Squirrel And The Ricketty Racketty Bridge'
Produced by Brian Eno

Obscure 9: Tom Phillips/Gavin Bryers – Irma
Tracks: 'An Introduction', 'Overture And Aria (I Tell You That's Irma Herself)', 'First Interlude', 'Aria (Irma You Will Be Mine)', 'Second Interlude', 'Chrous (Love Is Help Mate)', 'Postlude'
Produced by Brian Eno

Obscure 10: Harold Budd – The Pavilion of Dreams
Tracks: 'Bismillahi 'Rrahmani 'Rhahim', 'Two Songs: Let Us Go Into The House of the Lord', 'Butterfly Sunday (After The Rain)', 'Madrigals of the Rose Angel: Rosetti Noise', 'The Crystal Garden', 'Juno'

Obscure 11: Eno – Music for Airports
Produced by Eno
Recorded London, Cologne, 1978
Release date September 1978
Highest chart positions did not chart
Tracks: '1/1', '2/1', '1/2', '2/2'

There would be one final round of Obscure releases, by which time Eno clearly had other musical convolutions on his mind. Several artists whom Gavin Bryars felt very strongly would have benefitted the catalogue, were passed over (James Tenny and Martin Bartlett among them); Obscure already felt like a creature from another era. That said, several of Bryars' most important works were swept up across these albums.

Arguably the most remarkable of all the later Obscure releases, *Machine Music* features Bryars' 'The Squirrel And The Ricketty Racketty Bridge': a piece written for improvising guitarist Derek Bailey:

> Derek and I had worked together for a number of years, chiefly (plus Tony Oxley) with the trio Joseph Holbrooke. Derek's was one of the most important musical friendships of my life. In 1971, he asked me for a piece for the second album on his new Incus label, fully conscious, of course, that I had vehemently given up improvisation some five years earlier. I decided to make a piece that could not be something that might arise in his normal improvising, and so had him play two guitars at once, both lying flat on their backs. I also gave it some direct references to jazz, which is a word that Derek tried to avoid as much as possible.

Bryars, Bailey, Eno and Fred Frith are the featured players.

A founder member of the Promenade Theatre Orchestra and a leading light within the Scratch Orchestra, John White's contribution is magnificent minimalism. Four pieces each resolve to do as little as the attendant instruments could possibly accomplish short of remaining silent: a process that is nevertheless utterly captivating and absorbing. It is also best described (if not necessarily explained) by White's liner notes: 'I use the word 'machine' to define a consistent process governing a series of musical actions with a particular sound world, and by extension, the listener's perception thereof. One might thus regard the Welsh rarebit as a machine in which a process is applied to the conditioning and perception of the world of bread and cheese'.

Irma saw Bryars working with Tom Phillips: an artist he'd known since his return from the United States in 1968: 'He was among a number of composers in that experimental field, though Tom's work ultimately derived from, and was centred in, fine art. He was one of a number of musicians, like me, who taught in art colleges – I think he was the academic librarian at Wolverhampton Art College at that time. He was one of the composers who we published in the *Experimental Music Catalogue* when I took it over in 1972. Interestingly, Phillips was living next door to printmaker Ian Tyson at the same time as Eno was working for him'. A Phillips painting bedecks the cover of Eno's *Another Green World.*

Irma itself had a long history. Originally written in 1969, the opera was based upon a 19th-century novel (W. H. Mallock's *A Human Document*) purchased by Phillips from a secondhand book store and then, over the course of several years, gradually transformed into a whole new piece of art – *A Humument: A Treated Victorian Novel* – by means of painting, drawing, collaging and recreating the original book's actual pages. The resultant tome – closer now in spirit to a graphic novel than anything it originally resembled – was published in 1973 (and has been regularly reissued and expanded in the years since then), a year after the University of Newcastle staged the opera's UK premiere. Gavin Bryars: 'The idea of making a purely recorded version came through discussion with Brian about possible ideas, and I suggested making a realization from Tom's graphic notation. A score did exist as a single-page print, but it is not something that you could play from, as it only contains hints at notation'.

Accompanying a cast comprising Howard Skempton as Grenville, Lucy Skeaping as Irma, and Phillip and Angela Bryars in the chorus, an orchestra directed by Gavin Bryars seems to effortlessly capture the tones and directions of the original piece of art. It is a startling piece of work. But perhaps even more shocking was Phillips' own professed distaste for the completed work, resulting in a dispute between composer and artist that has only recently been resolved.

What became the final Obscure release was devoted to Harold Budd: destined to become one of Eno's regular conspirators, but another Gavin Bryars discovery. Like *Discrete Music* the first time around and the Penguin Cafe Orchestra in the second round of albums, *Pavilion of Dreams* swiftly ascended to popular acclaim.

But the label was finished. Although it was originally scheduled for release as Obscure 11, Eno's *Music for Airports* – engineered by Krautrock legend Conny Plank – would ultimately be delayed for six months before being released as the first album on a new, far more aptly-titled label: Ambient.

Chapter Eleven: Are You Customised?

February 1979: Roxy Music – 'Trash' b/w 'Trash 2' (Single)
March 1979: Roxy Music – Manifesto (Album)
Tracks: 'Manifesto', 'Trash', 'Angel Eyes', 'Still Falls The Rain', 'Stronger Through The Years', 'Ain't That So', 'My Little Girl', 'Dance Away', 'Cry, Cry, Cry', 'Spin Me Round'

April 1979: Roxy Music – 'Dance Away' b/w 'Cry, Cry, Cry' (Single)
August 1979: Roxy Music – 'Angel Eyes' b/w 'My Little Girl' (Single)
Personnel (all recordings):
Bryan Ferry: vocals, piano
Phil Manzanera: guitar
Andy Mackay: sax, horns
Paul Carrack: keyboards
Gary Tibbs: bass
Paul Thompson: drums
Produced by Roxy Music
Recorded 1978-79
LP release date: 16 March 1979
LP Highest Chart Positions
'Trash' release date 9 February 1979
'Trash' Highest Chart Positions UK: 40, US: did not chart
'Dance Away' release date 13 April, 1979
'Dance Away' Highest Chart Positions UK: 2, US: 44
'Angel Eyes' release date August 1979
'Angel Eyes' Highest Chart Positions UK: 4, US: did not chart

And after all that, they hadn't broken up after all. Or, if they had, they weren't admitting it now. Phil Manzanera even denied that Roxy Music had ever been a group, in the traditional sense. 'In terms of staying together', he told *Trouser Press*' Ira Robbins, 'at the end of this, we might go off and do something else for two years'.

Regardless, it was impossible not to feel a fission of excitement once the announcement of a new album was made; not to count down the days until the first single arrived; not to get up at the crack of dawn and score a copy immediately, lest Roxy should change their minds about the whole affair and break up again before breakfast. They didn't, and the sighs of relief were palpable. Not only were Roxy back, but they hadn't let us down either. 'Trash' truly was everything it should've been – playful, knowing, flirtatious, and granted a video that was as dynamic an introduction to the new-look band as their first film seven years before had welcomed us to the world of Roxy itself. In a club whose only audience appears to be shop-window dummies, Roxy are dressed dark but dangerous, with Ferry smiling the smile of a great white shark, and the band locked in doomstep around him. Only newly-recruited ex-Vibrators bassist Gary Tibbs breaks the mould: punky-styled and behaving a little like a puppy at a funeral. He learned fast, though – by the time the band appeared on Dutch TV's *TopPop*, he was as static as his bandmates, and it was the bubble machine that offered the most dramatic distraction.

And when you turned the disc over and listened to 'Trash 2' (aka 'Blue Trash'), there was the same song again, only this time it was slower, darker, even more sinister. An earlier Roxy might have pulled the two together and announced their return with almost six minutes of pleasure. And there was still time for them to do that because the album was another few weeks away. Ultimately though, they didn't do that, because *Manifesto* did not intend doing anything we thought – or even hoped – it might.

The sixth Roxy Music album is perhaps the group's most uncompromising record. Earlier albums – even their groundbreaking debut – had existed within the culture of their times, even as they rose above it. *Manifesto,* however, scarcely looked at what was happening around it, preferring instead to plot a course which was uniquely its own and uniquely Roxy Music. It was, indeed, a manifesto.

It had a disco tinge, but in many ways, that is evident only with hindsight. Similarly, comparisons can be made with the first two installments of Bowie/Eno's so-called Berlin trilogy: *Low* and *Heroes* (*Lodger* was still to follow). But 'Trash' dispensed with such role models with a shrug. And though the division of the album into two distinct halves (the dark dance of East; the lighter bounce of West) reeked of Berlin-esque artifice, even that device worked to its own specifications. And when 'Trash' turned out to not be the hit it deserved to be, Polydor were not dismayed. They simply turned to 'Dance Away' as a hasty follow-up. Radio loved it, dance floors flocked to it, and once the band had guested on Abba's BBC TV show (16 April: available on *The Thrill of it All),* suddenly Roxy Music were spiralling to the top of the dance charts.

When 'Angel Eyes' was re-recorded as a disco version, the die was cast – especially when paired to its accompanying video, festooned with a pair of windswept harp players all billowing scarves and fluffy hair, the pastel shading, and, oh dear, what *is* Bryan wearing today? Why, it's an early-1980s schoolgirl's wedding dress, cunningly time-slipped into suit form, and fitting him like a silken glove.

The re-recording was significant. On *Manifesto* – where 'Angel Eyes' appears on the East side – it was reminiscent of something from *Stranded*: alive with Mackay and Paul Carrack's bizarre interplay. Re-recorded, it became as frothy a love song as you could wish, and such was its success that *Manifesto* itself was re-pressed, replacing the original version of the song with what is now considered a trademark Roxy Music performance. The fact that the re-recording completely shatters the East side's feel, appeared to not have bothered anybody.

The greatest irony, however, lies in Roxy Music hurtling off on one tangent when there was another that they not only epitomised, but were largely responsible for in the first place. A host of newly-emergent bands – of whom Japan, Ultravox, Simple Minds and Gary Numan's Tubeway Army are just the first names out of the hat – all owed Roxy Music a considerable debt, and the acolytes weren't exclusively British. Across the pond, the likes of Devo and Pere Ubu (not to mention Television and Talking Heads) had likewise been staring through the old picture frame. And again, it's no coincidence that three of them had also been paired with producer Eno when, in at least one instance, Phil Manzanera might've been a far better match.

In so many ways and so many instances, as a new decade loomed closer, it could be argued that as much as David Bowie (and therefore more than anybody else whatsoever), Roxy Music had shaped whatever the 1980s were about to deliver, which is why they started to reshape themselves.

Manifesto's title track – which Ferry later described as the oldest idea on the record, but the last song to be recorded – is the perfect opener: stentorian and fierce; as confident a beginning as any past Roxy album ever boasted. 'Trash' follows, and that's a killer one-two. Next up, the original dark and dangerous 'Angel Eyes' – a brooding brute that did not in any shape or form deserve what was done to it in the name of filthy lucre. On and on *Manifesto* rolled, and, okay, the East side wiped the floor with the West, but we'd all heard a lot worse that year, and there was even worse to come. (Wasn't there, Mr Bowie?)

The press was less convinced than many fans. Ira Robbins at *Trouser Press* mused:

Manifesto hardly seems to be the worthy fulfilment of all the promises. As disappointing as some of the solo albums have been over the years, every Roxy Music LP (except for the lightweight Siren) has opened new vistas of musical surrealism. The basic failing of *Manifesto* is its lack of adventurousness; its failure to sound like nobody else. Though unmistakably Roxy Music, no track comes close to the joy of tunes like 'Do The Strand', 'The Thrill Of It All', 'All I Want Is You' or 'Both Ends Burning'. Played against the *Greatest Hits* album (a must-have for those unfamiliar with the band), *Manifesto* seems insubstantial.

Over at the *New Musical Express*, Max Bell wasn't even convinced by the East/West designations: '(It's) probably one of Brian's jokey red herrings, as the lyrical content may have more to do with the Fulham Road than the Great Wall of China, even if the title cut takes a polemical stand'. Politics and/or geography notwithstanding, Bell remained less than rapturous: 'For the moment, Ferry and his cohorts seem content to rely on tried-and-tested ethics, which may pall in the context they now find themselves in. Perhaps greater familiarity with *Manifesto* will reveal hidden magic. At present, it merely comes over like an assured modern dip into friendly territory: an entertaining, pleasant album'.

It was left to Richard Williams – the *Melody Maker* writer who had been documenting Roxy Music for longer than anyone – to look past the disappointments and see *Manifesto* for what it actually was, as opposed to what he wanted it to be.

Manifesto is a worthwhile attempt to make both form and content match its own internal preoccupations. It speaks of Ferry's continuing personal dilemma (which, put coarsely, boils down to the eternal choice between leather or tweed; between women who dare and women who care), and it wishes to satisfy those who bought 'Virginia Plain', while making genuflections to present-day American radio culture. Is it compromised by its emphasis on this double schizophrenia? Certainly, it pulls some punches. But, reservations aside, this may be the first such return bout ever attempted with any degree of genuine success: a technical knockout, against the odds.

And *still* nobody mentioned that there wasn't a scantily-clad lady on the cover.

12 April 1979: Roxy Music – Rainbow Music Hall, Denver (Album)

Personnel:
Bryan Ferry: vocals, piano
Phil Manzanera: guitar
Andy Mackay: sax, horns
David Skinner: keyboards
Gary Tibbs: bass
Paul Thompson: drums
Tracks: 'Manifesto', 'Angel Eyes', 'Trash', 'Out Of The Blue', 'A Song For Europe', 'Still Falls The Rain', 'Ain't That So', 'Stronger Through The Years', 'Ladytron', 'Every Dream Home A Heartache', 'Love Is The Drug', 'Do The Strand', 'Re-make/Re-model'
Bonus Tracks: 'Mother Of Pearl', 'Editions Of You' (Live in Oakland, 20 April)

Roxy Music returned to the road in February 1979.

24 February 1979 Isstadion, Stockholm, Sweden
04 March 1979 Grugahalle, Essen, Germany
05 March 1979 Carre, Amsterdam, Holland
06 March 1979 Congresgebouw The Hague, Holland
09 March 1979 Montreaux, Switzerland
11 March 1979 Pavillon de Paris, Porte de Pantin, France
13 March 1979 Halle Münsterland, Münster, Germany
14 March 1979 Jahrhunderthalle, Frankfurt, Germany
28 March 1979 Montgomery County Community College, Philadelphia PA
29 March 1979 Palladium, New York
30 March 1979 Tower Theatre, Philadelphia PA
31 March 1979 Orpheum Theatre, Boston, MA
01 April 1979 Towson University, Townson, MD
04 April 1979 Coliseum, Cleveland, OH
05 April 1979 Masonic Auditorium, Detroit, MI
06 April 1979 Uptown Theatre, Chicago, IL
08 April 1979 (unknown venue) Buffalo, NY
09 April 1979 (unknown venue) Columbus, OH
11 April 1979 Oriental Theatre, Milwaukee, WI
12 April 1979 Kiel Opera House, St Louis, MO
13 April 1979 One Block West, Kansas City, MO
14 April 1979 Guthrie Theater, Minneapolis, MN
15 April 1979 (unknown venue) Omaha City, NE

17 April 1979 Rainbow Music Hall, Denver, CO
20 April 1979 Oakland Auditorium, Oakland, CA
21 April 1979 Pasadena Civic, Pasadena, CA
22 April 1979 (unknown venue) San Diego, CA
26 April 1979 Nagoya City Hall, Nagoya, Japan
27 April 1979 Hesuteipa Hall, Osaka, Japan
28 April 1979 Budokan Hall, Tokyo, Japan

02 May 1979 De Montfort Hall, Leicester
03-04 May 1979 Odeon, Birmingham
06-07 May 1979 Apollo, Manchester
08-09 May 1979 Apollo, Glasgow
10-11 May 1979 City Hall, Newcastle
12 May 1979 Empire, Liverpool
13 May 1979 Hippodrome, Bristol
14 May 1979 Gaumont, Southampton
16-18 May 1979 Hammersmith Odeon, London

Television, radio and the ubiquitous bootleggers all awaited the reborn Roxy Music show, although highlights of the outing are preserved best on just two releases – the video *On The Road*, which captured Granada TV's footage of the Manchester show on 6 May (Highlights also appear on *The Thrill of it All*), and the syndicated US radio broadcast of the Denver gig, which had already circulated far and wide before it appeared in the quasi-legal *Concert Classics* series in 1998. (It has subsequently been reissued under a plethora of titles; still unofficial, but a fascinating document regardless.)

The same US tour also spawned the bootleg *Warped Leatherezz*, from the Oakland show. Its UK counterpart would be preserved on the unimaginatively titled *Hammersmith Odeon, 1979* boot.

Inevitably, *Manifesto* dominates the show. But it is clear too that Roxy know their legend as well as any – there's a healthy helping of crowd-pleasing oldies, but 'Love Is The Drug' is the sole concession to past hit singles. So while we can smile at the thought of the trendy young newcomers turning up in the hopes of hearing 'Dance Away', only to endure 'In Every Dream Home A Heartache' instead, nobody can accuse the band of throwing their past away. That said, the finest performances are reserved for the latest material – a seven-minute 'Stronger Through The Years' that appears to forget there's even an audience watching as it builds towards a segue into 'Ladytron', which itself is gifted a two-minute intro before Ferry starts to sing.

'Trash' is incredible, taken as fast as 'Trash 2' was taken slow, and so close to punk that the only way of stopping it is for Ferry to unleash a rooster impersonation at the end. Add the mania with which 'Editions Of You' and 'Mother Of Pearl' fly past, and we see how easy it would've been for Roxy to head off in an altogether opposite direction.

Epilogue: Who Knows What Tomorrow Might Bring?

Manifesto was not merely Roxy Music's last album of the 1970s; it was also the last that *sounded* like the Roxy Music of the 1970s, as Phil Manzanera reflected:

> There was a method of working which we had always used, which I can see now finished at the end of *Manifesto*. And when you change your method of working, you come up with something new. The way we made the records, completely changed ... From *Stranded* onwards, it had been a question of going into rehearsal with just four or five chords – no top-lines or anything like that – and playing the stuff around, then going and recording backing tracks, then overdubbing on top of the backing tracks, and then Bryan writing the top-line over those backing tracks, without anybody having any idea what the song was about, including Bryan at that stage. But from *Flesh and Blood* (1980) onwards, I had my studio up and running, and so the writing and the recording began happening simultaneously. It was all integrated and jumbled up, and that method of working led ultimately to *Avalon*, and it's a method of working which Bryan has continued with.

Flesh And Blood, from June 1980, is very much the anomaly in the Roxy Music catalogue. Given the group's traditional lack of permanency in the bass department, Gary Tibbs' departure to Adam and the Ants was perhaps only to be expected. The departure of drummer Paul Thompson, however, dealt the band a mortal blow, made all the more ironic by the fact that without him, Roxy Music would become even more popular than ever before. Thompson didn't care. Back in his native North-East, he told the local *Evening Chronicle*, 'I never went into this to make millions or become a star, it was always about the music. I didn't like the fame much – I remember coming out of filming *Top of The Pops* in the '70s, and girls were shouting and screaming for us. I just wanted to hide away. That sort of thing was never me. I just want to do what I do and enjoy it. As long as I can play and make enough money to survive, I'll be happy'.

Certainly, Thompson's absence was noticeable, all the more so since no permanent drummer would ever replace him. *Flesh And Blood* featured contributions from Allan Schwartzberg, Andy Newmark and ex-801er

Simon Phillips. (Thompson, meanwhile, went on to play with fellow Tynesiders Angelic Upstarts, and later, Concrete Blonde.)

But it was not only the feel of Roxy Music which was dramatically altered by Thompson's departure. The album's contents, too, were very much at odds with past group efforts. Repeating *Manifesto*'s record of producing three singles, *Flesh And Blood* also featured two cover versions – the first time the group, as opposed to individual members, had turned their attention to other artists' work: Wilson Pickett's 'In The Midnight Hour' and The Byrds' 'Eight Miles High'.

Covers continued on the band's mind later in the year too, when Roxy Music issued a studio version of John Lennon's 'Jealous Guy': a song which they had originally spontaneously included in a German television broadcast during the week of Lennon's assassination in December 1980. 'Jealous Guy' was released in a picture sleeve which simply stated, 'A Tribute', and students of British chart history will know the rest. Two successive Lennon singles – 'Imagine' and 'Woman' – topped the listings for the first six weeks of 1981; Joe Dolce's 'Shaddap Your Face' made an utterly irrelevant (but certainly mood-altering) appearance at the top in late February, and then Roxy Music powered in with what remains one of the longest singles that had yet topped the British chart. At over six minutes, only Queen's 'Bohemian Rhapsody' – and, of course, The Beatles' 'Hey Jude' – had hitherto boasted longer running times.

Roxy Music did not follow up 'Jealous Guy' for over a year. Instead, the only new release during 1981 was the somewhat ill-conceived British boxed set *The First Seven Albums*, which comprised just that – no unreleased material, no missing B-sides, not even a reprise of *Greatest Hits* to alleviate the absence of 'Virginia Plain'. Hardly surprisingly, it was all but ignored on release.

This latest lay-off, of course, again allowed the band members to exercise their own egos. Mackay wrote a book (*Electronic Music*), and Manzanera released the new solo album *Primitive Guitars* – itself essentially a listeners' guide to his technique and influences and entirely self-played and recorded, aside from a few bass lines provided by John Wetton. Nevertheless, it was worth hearing; indeed, anybody who has avoided this album after being burned by the distinctly AOR contents of the subsequent self-titled *Wetton/Manzanera* album (1987), should run and grab a copy now. It is nothing like what you are expecting!

Though it was completed sometime earlier, *Primitive Guitars* was released simultaneously with the new Roxy Music album *Avalon* in

May 1982: 'It was reviewed in *Rolling Stone* in the same review, which distressed Bryan incredibly', Manzanera laughs. 'I felt brilliant, I got a good review!'.

Previewed by the new single 'More Than This' – which reached number 6 in Britain – *Avalon* marked the culmination of Roxy Music's increasingly intense fascination with the studio (and was the blueprint for every subsequent Bryan Ferry solo disc!). Its rhapsodic feel, however, is totally at odds with the reports which leaked from the studios – of constant bickering between Ferry on the one part and Mackay and Manzanera on the other – as *Avalon* took its final form. Once again, the album was loaded down with singles – 'More Than This' was joined by the title track and 'Take A Chance With Me', while both 'India' (the instrumental B-side to 'More Than This') and 'To Turn You On' (the striking flip to 'Jealous Guy') won repeat appearances. Despite this, and despite *Avalon* itself being generally criticised for a certain (and undeniable) blandness, the album swiftly became Roxy Music's biggest-selling album yet, both at home and in the United States. It was, perhaps, only appropriate that the group should once again disband in its wake. However, could they have followed *Avalon*? Manzanera remembers:

> It was much like what happened after *Siren*. There was talk from the management saying Bryan wants to do another solo album, take another two years, and if it doesn't work... and this time we just said 'Fuck off', basically; 'We're going off to do our own thing'. There was no meeting where we all got together and said 'That's it'; no huge argument where somebody stormed out, nothing like that.

History repeats itself with almost monotonous accuracy. Just as *Siren* was succeeded by *Viva! Roxy Music*, so *Avalon* was followed a year later by a live recording, albeit a mere EP of four songs – *The High Road* – recorded on the band's final tour. Performances of 'Jealous Guy', and a breathtaking version of Neil Young's 'Like A Hurricane', were joined by 'My Only Love', and, surprisingly, a cut from Ferry's *The Bride Stripped Bare* album: 'Can't Let Go'. A full-length video of the same show was also released, its contents being duplicated on *Heart Still Beating*: a full-length album from the same tour's Frejus show, which was released in 1990. The band members themselves have reservations about this album, which appeared without any consultation. And, it is true, it is no *Viva! Roxy Music*. It is, nevertheless, a sterling example of the sheer majesty that Roxy Music was still capable of conjuring; any comparative weaknesses in the set are those that scarred the original albums from which the songs were taken.

Though Roxy Music was no more, the band members themselves continued to work. Unsurprisingly, Ferry was the first off the mark with 1984's *Boys and Girls* – still the finest of his self-penned solo albums – and alongside it, an epochal appearance at 1985's Live Aid concert. Subsequent Ferry albums have seldom touched the heights of that initial post-Roxy set, but they remain interesting if not exactly addictive. He is also still capable of springing the occasional surprise. He reunited with Eno, Manzanera and Mackay on 1994's *Mamouna*; cut a full album of Bob Dylan covers in 2007, and released two discs (2014's *The Jazz Age* and 2018's *Bitter-Sweet*) recasting both Roxy Music's and his own solo material in the style of a 1920s-era jazz band. At the time of writing, the latter remains his most recent solo release. *Avonmore*, in 2014, was his last album of new material.

Phil Manzanera too, has remained active in the years since *Avalon,* initially re-emerging alongside Andy Mackay in new band The Explorers, where the pair was joined by vocalist James Wraith: ex-Pete Brown's Flying Tigers. An exciting proposition, The Explorers were nevertheless sadly hamstrung by what the majority of listeners believed was Wraith's passing vocal resemblance to Bryan Ferry. The group's eponymous debut suffered accordingly but *does* reward the impartial listener, both through the material and a deceptively-strong sense of its own identity. Indeed, three decades on from its release, it is often hard to see what the comparisons were all about. And while *The Explorers* (and the four non-album singles which accompanied it) could be seen as a mere continuation of *Avalon*-era Roxy Music, it also stands proud as the new beginning which was never allowed to get started. Manzanera is stoical about The Explorers' failure: 'It's one of those things. After a few years of people saying James sounded like Bryan, we just gave up. He didn't to us, but he did to everyone else, so it was okay, we can't fight this, so we'd better give up'. (Incidentally, the American version of the album would not appear for another four years, when it was released credited to Mackay/Manzanera, and retitled *Up In Smoke*.)

Another self-titled Manzanera-Mackay album was released in 1990, again featuring Wraith on vocals, while Manzanera also launched his own label Expression Records. There he has maintained a constant steam of new releases under his own name. (The most recent at the time of writing was 2021's *Caught by the Heart*, pairing him with Tim Finn.)

He has also established himself as curator of Roxy's extracurricular catalogue, overseeing reissues of numerous projects by himself and Andy Mackay, including 801, The Explorers and Quiet Sun. Away from all that, Manzanera was co-producer of David Gilmour's *In An Island* (2006) and *Rattle That* Lock (2015) albums and was a key component within Gilmour's live band.

Andy Mackay has been less prolific. His most recent release – 2018's *3 Psalms* – was only his fifth solo record. Paul Thompson, too has faded from the public eye.

But even amidst so much activity, the Roxy Music story was not over: not on the shelves – where regular hits collections were joined by the *The Thrill of it All* box set – and not in person either. The first *reunion* took place in the summer of 1995. On that occasion, it came to naught. Manzanera reflected shortly after:

> There's certainly a lot of interest, but it's one of those things, you can never really tell. We almost got together and recorded something, but because of business hassles, it didn't happen, and it's sort of on/off the whole time. But really, I feel a little bit ambivalent about it, because on the one hand it would be great if it worked and the public – just like I do for other bands – will say 'Great, love to see you back together'. But then I go to concerts of bands I wanted to see back together, and I come away disappointed, and ask why did they bother? If it was brilliant, I'd love it. But if it isn't, or if we don't deliver anything worthwhile, and we end our career on a complete downer, I don't want to. At the moment, it's completely preserved, finishing with Avalon, because that was a good album, and started off with a good album; a neat career. The other thing is, okay, which Roxy? The first one, the middle one or the last one? And then you wonder, is any of it relevant in the 1990s? And by the time you've answered all those questions, you almost think 'Forget it'.

Almost... but never forever. Six years later, in February 2001, Roxy Music announced a world tour: opening in Dublin before moving to the UK and thence across Europe. The United States and Canada would follow. Ferry, Manzanera, Mackay and Thompson represented the original lineup, and while no new album was planned, there would be both a live album and a live DVD. And whether you caught the band in person or hung on for *Roxy Music Live at the Apollo*, there was little doubt that Roxy Music could still put on a great show.

That was not the end. Manzanera and Thompson regrouped with Ferry for his 2002 *Frantic* album (Eno also featured on one track) and the accompanying tour. And in 2005, Roxy Music appeared at the Isle of Wight Festival and at the German segment of the Live 8 concert. That same year, Phil Manzanera's website reported that a new album *was* finally in the air, and would feature contributions from Eno too. The following year – with health issues having forced Thompson to be replaced by Andy Newmark – Roxy Music toured Europe, and in 2007, Ferry too confirmed that the album was on its way. It didn't show up. But there was more live work in 2010, including a host of festivals, with Thompson returning to the lineup for all but three of these (Andy Newmark again stood in for him). The following year brought visits to Australia and New Zealand and a short UK tour. And then, silence.

Ferry's solo career continued apace; Manzanera's too. Mackay and Thompson reunited in a new project: The Metaphors. Life went on. It would be another three years before Manzanera admitted to *Rolling Stone* that Roxy Music was finished. He explained the band had just come off stage following their appearance at the O2 Arena in London on 7 February 2011 when he and Mackay looked at one another and said, 'Our job here is done'.

The reviews agreed. As *The Independent* put it, 'Only quite late on in the evening, somewhere between Bryan Ferry's plaintive whistle in 'Jealous Guy' and the longed-for intro to 'Virginia Plain', is Roxy Music's O2 audience roused to something like excitement. It's clearly a huge relief to Ferry, but it's the band's own fault – with as elegantly-innovative a back catalogue as Roxy's, this should have been a torrent of exuberant memories. But for substantial portions of the set, the longueurs are alleviated only by the consistently exciting guitar work'.

Manzanera continued: 'Musicians like to do new things'. But he agreed, 'It's unfortunate for the fans'.

Indeed it was. But at least there was still the new album to look forward to… wasn't there? No. That too had been scrapped, he continued to *Rolling Stone*: 'We all listened to it and thought, 'We can't do this. It's not going to be any good. Let's just bin it'. And so it's just sitting there on our personal computers. Maybe one day it'll get finished. But there's no point in putting it out if it's not great'.

There has been just one sighting since then, when Roxy Music were inducted into the Rock and Roll Hall of Fame in 2019, with Ferry, Mackay, Manzanera and Eddie Jobson reuniting for a six-song set. Instead, attention turned to something else Manzanera had spoken of earlier in the decade: deluxe box-set versions of 1972's *Roxy Music* (finally released in 2018) and *For Your Pleasure.*

We're still waiting for the latter, but Roxy Music fans are nothing if not patient. In fact, if they did anything when you were expecting them to, they wouldn't be Roxy Music - a point that was proved just days before this book went to press, when it was announced that the Ferry, Mackay, Manzanera, Thompson core was reuniting for a 50th-anniversary tour.

It's a brief outing - nine dates across the United States, one in Canada and three in the UK. But what do you expect? Like the song said all those years ago, the trees were taller, the grass was greener and the heels were higher when we were young. The tours were longer, too.

On Track series

Alan Parsons Project – Steve Swift 978-1-78952-154-2

Tori Amos – Lisa Torem 978-1-78952-142-9

Asia – Peter Braidis 978-1-78952-099-6

Badfinger – Robert Day-Webb 978-1-878952-176-4

Barclay James Harvest – Keith and Monica Domone 978-1-78952-067-5

The Beatles – Andrew Wild 978-1-78952-009-5

The Beatles Solo 1969-1980 – Andrew Wild 978-1-78952-030-9

Blue Oyster Cult – Jacob Holm-Lupo 978-1-78952-007-1

Blur – Matt Bishop – 978-178952-164-1

Marc Bolan and T.Rex – Peter Gallagher 978-1-78952-124-5

Kate Bush – Bill Thomas 978-1-78952-097-2

Camel – Hamish Kuzminski 978-1-78952-040-8

Caravan – Andy Boot 978-1-78952-127-6

Cardiacs – Eric Benac 978-1-78952-131-3

Eric Clapton Solo – Andrew Wild 978-1-78952-141-2

The Clash – Nick Assirati 978-1-78952-077-4

Crosby, Stills and Nash – Andrew Wild 978-1-78952-039-2

The Damned – Morgan Brown 978-1-78952-136-8

Deep Purple and Rainbow 1968-79 – Steve Pilkington 978-1-78952-002-6

Dire Straits – Andrew Wild 978-1-78952-044-6

The Doors – Tony Thompson 978-1-78952-137-5

Dream Theater – Jordan Blum 978-1-78952-050-7

Electric Light Orchestra – Barry Delve 978-1-78952-152-8

Elvis Costello and The Attractions – Georg Purvis 978-1-78952-129-0

Emerson Lake and Palmer – Mike Goode 978-1-78952-000-2

Fairport Convention – Kevan Furbank 978-1-78952-051-4

Peter Gabriel – Graeme Scarfe 978-1-78952-138-2

Genesis – Stuart MacFarlane 978-1-78952-005-7

Gentle Giant – Gary Steel 978-1-78952-058-3

Gong – Kevan Furbank 978-1-78952-082-8

Hall and Oates – Ian Abrahams 978-1-78952-167-2

Hawkwind – Duncan Harris 978-1-78952-052-1

Peter Hammill – Richard Rees Jones 978-1-78952-163-4

Roy Harper – Opher Goodwin 978-1-78952-130-6

Jimi Hendrix – Emma Stott 978-1-78952-175-7

The Hollies – Andrew Darlington 978-1-78952-159-7

Iron Maiden – Steve Pilkington 978-1-78952-061-3

Jefferson Airplane – Richard Butterworth 978-1-78952-143-6

Jethro Tull – Jordan Blum 978-1-78952-016-3

Elton John in the 1970s – Peter Kearns 978-1-78952-034-7

The Incredible String Band – Tim Moon 978-1-78952-107-8

Iron Maiden – Steve Pilkington 978-1-78952-061-3

Judas Priest – John Tucker 978-1-78952-018-7

Kansas – Kevin Cummings 978-1-78952-057-6

The Kinks – Martin Hutchinson 978-1-78952-172-6

Korn – Matt Karpe 978-1-78952-153-5

Led Zeppelin – Steve Pilkington 978-1-78952-151-1

Level 42 – Matt Philips 978-1-78952-102-3

Little Feat – 978-1-78952-168-9

Aimee Mann – Jez Rowden 978-1-78952-036-1

Joni Mitchell – Peter Kearns 978-1-78952-081-1

The Moody Blues – Geoffrey Feakes 978-1-78952-042-2

Motorhead – Duncan Harris 978-1-78952-173-3

Mike Oldfield – Ryan Yard 978-1-78952-060-6

Opeth – Jordan Blum 978-1-78-952-166-5

Tom Petty – Richard James 978-1-78952-128-3

Porcupine Tree – Nick Holmes 978-1-78952-144-3

Queen – Andrew Wild 978-1-78952-003-3

Radiohead – William Allen 978-1-78952-149-8

Renaissance – David Detmer 978-1-78952-062-0

The Rolling Stones 1963-80 – Steve Pilkington 978-1-78952-017-0

The Smiths and Morrissey – Tommy Gunnarsson 978-1-78952-140-5

Status Quo the Frantic Four Years – Richard James 978-1-78952-160-3

Steely Dan – Jez Rowden 978-1-78952-043-9

Steve Hackett – Geoffrey Feakes 978-1-78952-098-9

Thin Lizzy – Graeme Stroud 978-1-78952-064-4

Toto – Jacob Holm-Lupo 978-1-78952-019-4

U2 – Eoghan Lyng 978-1-78952-078-1
UFO – Richard James 978-1-78952-073-6
The Who – Geoffrey Feakes 978-1-78952-076-7
Roy Wood and the Move – James R Turner 978-1-78952-008-8
Van Der Graaf Generator – Dan Coffey 978-1-78952-031-6
Yes – Stephen Lambe 978-1-78952-001-9
Frank Zappa 1966 to 1979 – Eric Benac 978-1-78952-033-0
Warren Zevon – Peter Gallagher 978-1-78952-170-2
10CC – Peter Kearns 978-1-78952-054-5

Decades Series

The Bee Gees in the 1960s – Andrew Mon Hughes et al
978-1-78952-148-1
The Bee Gees in the 1970s – Andrew Mon Hughes et al
978-1-78952-179-5
Black Sabbath in the 1970s – Chris Sutton 978-1-78952-171-9
Britpop – Peter Richard Adams and Matt Pooler 978-1-78952-169-6
Alice Cooper in the 1970s – Chris Sutton 978-1-78952-104-7
Curved Air in the 1970s – Laura Shenton 978-1-78952-069-9
Bob Dylan in the 1980s – Don Klees 978-1-78952-157-3
Fleetwood Mac in the 1970s – Andrew Wild 978-1-78952-105-4
Focus in the 1970s – Stephen Lambe 978-1-78952-079-8
Free and Bad Company in the 1970s – John Van der Kiste
978-1-78952-178-8
Genesis in the 1970s – Bill Thomas 978178952-146-7
George Harrison in the 1970s – Eoghan Lyng 978-1-78952-174-0
Marillion in the 1980s – Nathaniel Webb 978-1-78952-065-1
Mott the Hoople and Ian Hunter in the 1970s – John Van der Kiste
978-1-78-952-162-7
Pink Floyd In The 1970s – Georg Purvis 978-1-78952-072-9
Tangerine Dream in the 1970s – Stephen Palmer 978-1-78952-161-0
The Sweet in the 1970s – Darren Johnson 978-1-78952-139-9
Uriah Heep in the 1970s – Steve Pilkington 978-1-78952-103-0
Yes in the 1980s – Stephen Lambe with David Watkinson 978-1-78952-125-2

On Screen series

Carry On... – Stephen Lambe 978-1-78952-004-0
David Cronenberg – Patrick Chapman 978-1-78952-071-2
Doctor Who: The David Tennant Years – Jamie Hailstone 978-1-78952-066-8
James Bond – Andrew Wild – 978-1-78952-010-1
Monty Python – Steve Pilkington 978-1-78952-047-7
Seinfeld Seasons 1 to 5 – Stephen Lambe 978-1-78952-012-5

Other Books

1967: A Year In Psychedelic Rock – Kevan Furbank 978-1-78952-155-9
1970: A Year In Rock – John Van der Kiste 978-1-78952-147-4
1973: The Golden Year of Progressive Rock 978-1-78952-165-8
Babysitting A Band On The Rocks – G.D. Praetorius 978-1-78952-106-1
Eric Clapton Sessions – Andrew Wild 978-1-78952-177-1
Derek Taylor: For Your Radioactive Children – Andrew Darlington
978-1-78952-038-5
The Golden Road: The Recording History of The Grateful Dead – John
Kilbride 978-1-78952-156-6
Iggy and The Stooges On Stage 1967-1974 – Per Nilsen 978-1-78952-101-6
Jon Anderson and the Warriors – the road to Yes – David Watkinson
978-1-78952-059-0
Nu Metal: A Definitive Guide – Matt Karpe 978-1-78952-063-7
Tommy Bolin: In and Out of Deep Purple – Laura Shenton
978-1-78952-070-5
Maximum Darkness – Deke Leonard 978-1-78952-048-4
Maybe I Should've Stayed In Bed – Deke Leonard 978-1-78952-053-8
The Twang Dynasty – Deke Leonard 978-1-78952-049-1

and many more to come!

Peter Gabriel - *on track*
every album, every song

Graeme Scarfe
Paperback
160 pages
40 colour photographs
978-178-952-138-2
£14.99
USD 21.95

**Every album recorded
by this British pioneer
of progressive music.**

If Genesis, according to British comedian and fan Al Murray 'were the progressive rock band who progressed', then Peter Gabriel as a solo artist would be the member that progressed the most. Who would have thought that listening to early Genesis would eventually take the listener to Senegal, Armenia, South Africa and beyond, via the artistic endeavours of their former vocalist?

This is a journey through Peter Gabriel's solo albums, his live recordings and soundtrack compositions. During his forty-year plus solo career, Gabriel has become a worldwide pop star via his early, self-titled albums and his seminal 1986 record

So. He has had hit singles throughout his career, including the bucolic 'Solsbury Hill' in 1977 and the poignant 'Don't Give Up'. He also helped pioneer video creativity with the song 'Sledgehammer'. In doing so, he has reached beyond his progressive rock origins to achieve a level of popularity and respect that other musicians from that genre could only dream about. You may have heard many of these songs before, but there's always something new to be found by digging in the dirt. This is the perfect guide to his music for new listeners and long-term fans alike.

What on earth is going on? In the words of the Burgermiester: 'I...will...find...out.'

Yes in the 80s
Decades

Stephen Lambe with David
Watkinson
Paperback
192 pages
80 colour photographs
978-178-952-125-2
£16.99
USD 24.95

**An in-depth
examination of this
famous progressive
rock band's most
turbulent decade.**

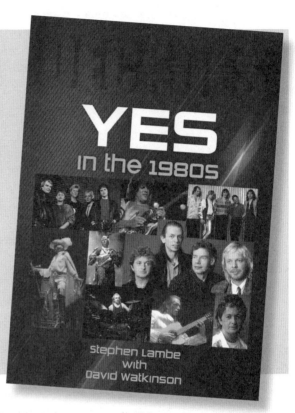

When Yes ran into problems recording their tenth album in Paris at the end of 1979, it was almost the end. Yet in the 1980s, the band rallied, firstly as part of an unlikely collaboration with new wave duo The Buggles, then with *90125*, the most successful album of their career, which spawned a number one hit in the USA with 'Owner Of A Lonely Heart'. The band failed to capitalise on this success, however, lingering too long over its successor *Big Generator* and by the end of the decade, Yes had effectively split into two versions of the same group.

With most authors concentrating on the group's 1970s career, *Yes in the*

1980s looks in forensic detail at this relatively underexamined era of the band's history, featuring rarely-seen photos researched by author David Watkinson. The book follows the careers of all nine significant members of the group during a turbulent decade which saw huge highs but also many lows. Not only does it consider the three albums the band itself made across the decade, but also the solo careers and other groups – including Asia, XYZ, The Buggles, Jon and Vangelis and GTR - formed by those musicians as the decade wound towards a reunion of sorts in the early 1990s.

Would you like to write for Sonicbond Publishing?

At Sonicbond Publishing we are always on the look-out for authors, particularly for our two main series:

On Track. Mixing fact with in depth analysis, the On Track series examines the work of a particular musical artist or group. All genres are considered from easy listening and jazz to 60s soul to 90s pop, via rock and metal.

On Screen. This series looks at the world of film and television. Subjects considered include directors, actors and writers, as well as entire television and film series. As with the On Track series, we balance fact with analysis.

While professional writing experience would, of course, be an advantage the most important qualification is to have real enthusiasm and knowledge of your subject. First-time authors are welcomed, but the ability to write well in English is essential.

Sonicbond Publishing has distribution throughout Europe and North America, and all books are also published in E-book form. Authors will be paid a royalty based on sales of their book.

Further details are available from www.sonicbondpublishing.co.uk. To contact us, complete the contact form there or email info@sonicbondpublishing.co.uk